SURFER

^{RM}

lume Ten ∎ Number One ∎ March ∎ 75 Cents

A BRIEF HISTORY OF SURFING

BY MATT WARSHAW

CHRONICLE BOOKS
SAN FRANCISCO

Page 267 constitutes a continuation
of the copyright page.

Library of Congress Cataloging-in-Publication
Data available.

ISBN: 978-1-4521-5194-6

Manufactured in China.

FSC
www.fsc.org

MIX
Paper from
responsible sources
FSC™ C104723

Designed by Ben Kither

10 9 8 7 6 5 4 3 2 1

Chronicle Books LLC
680 Second Street
San Francisco, CA 94107

Page 1: Sam Hawk.
Page 2: Dusty Payne.
Page 3: Corky Carroll.
Page 4: Tom Blake and Santa Monica lifeguards.
Page 5: Detail from 1968 *Surfer* magazine cover.
Page 6-7: Palos Verdes Cove.
Above: Hobie Surfboards shop.
Page 276: Midget Farrelly.

www.chroniclebooks.com

CONTENTS

INTRODUCTION

By Matt Warshaw

The original *History of Surfing* was my
attempt to clean-and-jerk the entire gor-
geous, sprawling mess of a sport, to hoist
it up where surfers and nonsurfers alike
could see it anew and in full. I hoped to
add verity to the record. For instance,
remember those beautifully lacquered,
solid-wood, Depression-era surfboards?
For decades, received wisdom was that
they weighed a knee-buckling 100 pounds.
Pick up a hundred pounds of anything
and walk from one end of the block to
the other. Now imagine doing the same
thing before and after every surf session.
Equipment that heavy might not have
killed the sport outright, but it would have
dragged it down considerably. As it turns
out, the average board made in the 1930s
weighed about 50 pounds. Does it change
anything, or lessen the sport's achievements, to deflate little surf-world myths
like this? Maybe, a little, but it's the truth.
And even so—fifty pounds is still pretty
damn heavy.

Demythologizing the sport, in fact,
was another goal of mine. I couldn't wait
to sledge away at the cheerleading and
boosterism and perjured nobility layered
onto most works of surf history. Pulling
down shoddy historiographic handicraft
feels good, just for its own sake. But the
real purpose—and the real pleasure—
comes from the fact that the mortal,
ground-level version of events is, almost
without exception, more compelling than

the legend or the myth. Surfing history has time and again been presented for two reasons: to convince nonsurfers that riding waves is an honest-to-goodness sport, rather than a beachfront novelty, and to reassure surfers themselves that their days and years spent chasing down swells is not only justified but virtuous—that their chosen recreation is in fact more of a calling. The rest of the world now thinks surfing is great. Fine. No harm there. The second part, though, has done the sport a disservice. Let's revel in surfing's grace and beauty, and applaud the surfer's bravery, innovation, and humor. Absolutely. But let's also acknowledge the sexism, the pettiness, the hubris, and all the other messy human qualities that are stitched and glued into the sport's fabric. Leave room for second thoughts. One of my favorite quotes about the surfing life comes from Hawaii's Ken Bradshaw. Invariably portrayed as a brash, disciplined surfwarrior—and celebrated in the late 1990s as the man who'd ridden the biggest wave in the sport's history up to that point— Bradshaw mused late in his career about "all the opportunities I missed because I'm so obsessively addicted to surfing." He then added: "Don't be me. I don't have what most human beings want."

Not for a moment do I think that Bradshaw, if given the chance, would really change his life or career. His ride has been long and thrilling and steeped in glory. Only when he reckons the cost of his all-encompassing pursuit, though, does he become a three-dimensional human being, rather than a two-dimensional stock character. What's true for Bradshaw

is true for the sport. Surf history is better when it's not moonlighting as surf advocacy. Surfing is more clearly seen, and more authentically honorable, when it steps off its pedestal.

I turned in a final draft for the original *History of Surfing* in mid-2009, after four years of research and writing. Throughout, I was half-waiting for a surfworld epiphany or two to land on me. It never happened. But my biases and preferences all came through intact. Today, the mechanics of surfboard design, and all the attendant hydrodynamics, still bore me just as much as the forces *behind* design change—the rivalries, the spark of an idea, trial and error, dumb luck—still fascinate me. It's the same with surf competition. While I consider 90-some percent of surf contests to be silly distractions, the best events and the top competitors can distill a moment in the sport like nothing else. Nat Young's amazing performance in the 1966 World Championships in San Diego was like hearing the thunder from the coming shortboard revolution almost a full year before it came into view. In the end, board design and competition both receive prominent roles in this history because, as often as not, they're the quickest, most efficient route to the sport's most interesting places.

What really attracts me, though, is tracing and understanding the jagged fault line between surf culture and culture at large. It's running down simple things like the etymology of "dude," as well as following longer, episodic storylines: how Kathy "Gidget" Kohner went from an unknown fifteen-year-old Malibu mascot to the subject of a hit movie, which in turn put an entire generation of new surfers in the water—most of whom decided to hate *Gidget* as a surf-Eden destroyer, until they later came to love the film as a memento of their beachgoing youth. Almost every inch in this particular acre of surf history is deliciously fraught with morality plays, from the small and personal—Malibu antihero Mickey Dora selling out to the *Beach Blanket Bingo* franchise, for example—to the socially charged, like the pro surfing tour's decision to hold contests in apartheid-era South Africa.

The nonsurfing world has shaped and formed the sport more deeply than surfers care to admit. Surf culture, in turn, has traveled and settled over mountains, plains, and cities, from coast to coast, nation to nation. For me, watching these two forces react to each other never gets dull: the circling and grinding and ignoring and ridiculing—and, these days, more often than not, collaborating.

Former world champion Fred Hemmings's belief is that surfing, for the most part, is nothing more than "a clean, healthy *S-P-O-R-T*." I wouldn't argue the point. A version of surf history can in good faith be told mostly in terms of athletic achievement and the sport's advances in equipment and technique. But that makes for a flat, narrow portrait. So many other narratives—equally important and a lot more colorful—have to be accounted for, most of them having little or nothing to do with sport. They involve Hollywood, politics, music, fashion, and the brave new digital vastness. ("Surf the fucking net indeed," an Australian surfer wrote with

righteous disdain in 1999, the nonsurfing world having gone one appropriation too far. "Give us back our verb!") Mostly, though, athletic terms alone can never adequately explain the abiding fanaticism—from mild to deranged, both ridiculous and sublime—that to such a large degree has defined the character and history of surfing. Hemmings is right. Surfing is a sport. But it's not just a sport. To one degree or another, I am also persuaded by those who cast their view of wave-riding into the near and far regions of art, religion, philosophy, and metaphysics. Hemmings's sport is somebody else's return to the briny comfort of the womb. Or their mortal imitation of Jesus's walk on water. Or meditation. Or modern dance. At the very least, this rush to load a pretty straightforward recreational act with meaning puts a light on the towering level of devotion surfing inspires. Except it often feels like more than that. Veteran surf journalist Matt George, a friend of mine for over forty years, once said that our drive to ride waves re-creates the amoebic sea-to-land dash through the Paleozoic shorebreak and allows us to "touch the elemental magma of our souls." My response in the late eighties, when I first read that, was to laugh out loud. Now I smile and shrug and think it's just an alternative (if slightly purple) way to express something I also feel.

The last and most important thing I hoped to accomplish with *The History of Surfing* was to make room for all the different kinds of people who've been attracted to wave-riding through the decades, to let the full cast of characters have a turn front and center. True, the Brief History you're holding in your hands means that everybody gets less time up there. But still, I've tried to stretch it out to include everyone from diehard sportsman to soul-magma proselytizer. Waves animate surfing. But surfers make it interesting.

A NOTE ON WAVE MEASUREMENT

Purposely downplaying wave height became a standard surf-world practice in the late 1960s. Before that, surfers generally tried to give an honest appraisal, measuring from crest to trough at the wave's peak height. If anything, they exaggerated. Once the trendsetting Hawaiians began to reduce their estimates, however, particularly with regard to large waves—showing a dismissive cool toward a watery environment that was pretty much terrifying to everyone else, non-Hawaiian surfers included—it was just a matter of time before the rest of the sport fell in line. Soon, a wave described as eight feet on the "Hawaiian scale" was in reality over double the height of what surfers from 1959 would have called an eight-footer. Surfers would still describe a wave's actual size, but they prefaced the number with "face height" or "on the face" to signal that it wasn't the *real* height according to the Hawaiian scale. It was all pretty silly.

Meanwhile, a lot of numbers were dropped from the wave-height lexicon altogether. There was no such thing as a nine-foot wave. Or an eleven-, thirteen-, or fourteen-foot wave. Starting at twenty feet, the measurements came only in five-foot increments. These were all surf-world traditions by the early 1970s.

In the nineties, not long after big-wave riders began using Jet Skis to catch waves half-again bigger than anything previously ridden, the trough-to-crest measurement made a comeback. The idea now was to quantifiably dramatize the difference between old- and new-generation big-wave surfing, and estimates were once again made to the foot. After much deliberation, a panel of surfing experts declared Makua Rothman's winning wave in the 2002 XXL Big Wave competition to be precisely sixty-six feet. Also, online surf reports and forecasts, hoping to standardize the metric, began reporting "face height."

Both systems remain in use as of 2017, but a vast majority of surfers—so far resisting the efforts of surf forecasters—still measure waves at somewhere between 50 and 75 percent of their face height. This book, too, defaults to the Hawaiian scale. Whenever possible, I've tried to make the whole thing a little easier by skipping numbers altogether and using terms like "waist-high," "head-high," or "double-overhead," and so on.

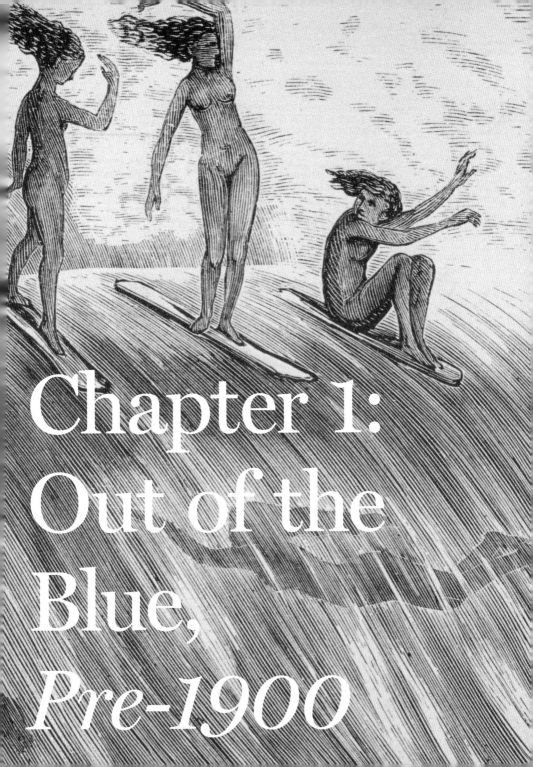

Chapter 1: Out of the Blue, Pre-1900

Fisherman along the coast of what is now Peru were likely riding waves more than three thousand years ago using a woven-reed vessel called the *caballito,* or "little horse." The *caballito* is still in use; roughly 12 feet long and 90 pounds, a fisherman will paddle it out through the surf using a bamboo paddle, drop a line, and fill a rear compartment with the catch of the day. The *caballito* is a tool designed for the serious, tedious business of feeding the community. At some point, though, in all likelihood sooner rather than later, the fluttery thrill of riding a wave on the way back to the beach became its own reward. Who knows? Perhaps this easily repeatable and wholly nonproductive act was removed from the daily work routine and pursued for its own sake. A form of surfing began. The original form.

That's how a handful of surf-world *caballistas* view it, anyway. Most surfers don't see it that way. None of the evidence proves that wave-riding in ancient Peru developed into an established, widespread form of recreation. Weather alone argues against it—for most of the year, beachfront air and water temperatures in Peru are prohibitively cold. This doesn't mean that generations of pre-Columbian fishermen didn't enjoy their daily free ride to shore. They were wired just like us, and swift, semicontrolled motion always pays off with a nice hit of adrenaline.

In fact, it's easy to imagine that wave-riding in one form or another likely took root on antediluvian beaches from Brazil to Senegal, Lebanon to Borneo. Modern surfing was born in Hawaii, but for any ancestral society living on a temperate coastline, riding waves would likely have been a natural, perhaps intuitive act. Dolphins and pelicans seem to do it purely out of enjoyment, after all. When did the first human wade into the shorebreak and try to imitate a dolphin? Or put another way—when did bodysurfing start? That probably goes back millions of years, not thousands.

A CABALLITO-RIDING FISHERMAN RETURNS TO THE BEACH AT HUANCHACO, PERU.

ANCIENT HAWAII, PART I

The history of modern surfing is directly and organically connected to Polynesia—specifically Hawaii. Unlike ancient Peru, where wave-riding was a by-product of work and probably limited to fishermen, surfing in Hawaii was both recreational and universal. Polynesians first arrived in Hawaii around 300 AD, bringing with them a rudimentary form of surfing that developed in Hawaii into a communal obsession. The ruling class had special boards and exclusive breaks, but even so, the sport became the island nation's great common denominator. Surfing was practiced with equal enthusiasm (and class-leveling nudity) by farmers, warriors, weavers, healers, fishermen, children, grandparents, chiefs, and regents. As one early Western visitor wrote, "The entire population of a village would at certain hours resort to the sea-side to indulge in, or to witness, this magnificent accomplishment."

Warfare was a regular part of ancient Hawaiian society, but day-to-day life was filled with languor and play. Relationships between sport, religion, myth, work, war, family, and courtship were fluid, and surfing came to be entwined with almost all aspects of life. Priests whipped the nearshore waters with long vines in order to bring the surf up. Artists carved petroglyph stick-figure images of surfers onto flat lava surfaces. Laborers built terraced oceanfront shrines where surfers could rinse off after exiting the water or pray for waves if the surf was flat.

FIRST PUBLISHED SURFING IMAGE, 1831.

Surfing in ancient Hawaii was fused to sex, competition, and gambling. A pair of would-be lovers riding side by side for more than two or three waves did so in the knowledge that they'd taken their flirtation to a level that practically demanded a beeline for the beach and a quick damp-skinned coupling in the nearest available hut or glade. During a big surfing competition among royals, crowds lined the beach and squinted out to the wave zone, many of them with that expression of rapture and dread common to hard-core gamblers everywhere. Hawaiians would stake anything from a fishing net and a chicken or two to swine, a canoe, or indentured servitude—life itself, in a rare few cases—on a contest's outcome. Competitors all wore a special loincloth dyed brilliant red, and between rides they kept their strength up by snacking on roasted dog, specially prepared that day in an underground oven. Women surfed against men, and as a nineteenth-century native-born writer noted, "The gentler sex [often] carried off the highest honors." As the surfers took their place in the lineup, the roar that went up—a combination of shouts, taunts, laughter, and endless spontaneous wagering—made the event seem more like a boxing match than an afternoon at the beach.

PRIOR TO CONTACT WITH THE WESTERN WORLD, AND OFTEN IN THE DECADES THAT FOLLOWED, HAWAIIANS DID THEIR SURFING IN THE NUDE.

THE ALAIA SURFBOARD

Surfing as the world knows it was for all practical purposes invented on the alaia, a midsize board about 6 or 7 feet long, round at the nose, tapered and squared-off at the tail, slightly convex along the bottom, less than 2 inches thick, and weighing about 45 pounds. The alaia "vibrates against the rider's abdomen, chest, [and] hands," a nineteenth-century Hawaiian noted, describing the sensitive ride of such a thin craft. The alaia was the Hawaiian standard, used by monarchs and villagers alike; it paddled well enough to catch waves before they spilled over, but was responsive and maneuverable enough to let the surfer ride in the steep, fast, curling section of the wave. Without a stabilizing fin, the alaia provided only limited control, so that performance was judged less on the route taken across the wave, as with today's surfing, and more on the rider's style. The best surfers moved smoothly from position to position: belly down, kneeling, sitting, and hardest of all, standing. They also rode at an angle to the wave face, just ahead of the whitewater, doubling or even tripling their speed compared to the novice surfer heading straight for the beach. Expertise was demonstrated in other ways. At the south end of Kealakekua Bay, on the Big Island, where lava outcroppings spill off the beach into the water, part of the game was to finish off a ride by shooting through gaps in the nearshore rocks. Pulling back at the last moment, as one early Western observer noted, was not only "reckoned very disgraceful," but often led to "the loss of the board, which I have often seen, with great horror, dashed to pieces at the very moment the islander quitted it."

LATE-NINETEENTH-CENTURY BIG ISLAND SURFERS WITH ALAIA BOARDS.

THE "DISCOVERY" OF HAWAII

First contact between Hawaii and the West was initiated in 1778, when Captain James Cook, of England, island-hopped from Kauai to Niihau to the Big Island. It's hard to imagine two more culturally divergent groups of people than the Hawaiians and the British visitors: the grimy loom-woven canvas sailor's outfits and the islanders' casual nudity; Christianity's solitary, white-bearded God in Heaven and Hawaii's crowded soap-opera cast of spirits and deities. Wave-riding was also part of the disparity. During Cook's time, therapeutic "sea bathing" was a minor health craze among Great Britain's upper classes, but for the overwhelming majority of Westerners, the ocean was a place (as Shakespeare put it) of "dead men's skulls" and "a thousand fearful wrecks." For all his extraordinary seagoing accomplishments, Captain Cook remained a product of his water-averse generation, and like virtually all of his fellow British mariners, he didn't know how to swim. Also, in accordance with Old Testament teachings on nature in general, Cook viewed the ocean as a dangerous force badly in need of conquering. Few things in his worldwide travels likely surprised him more than the idea of playing in the surf.

FIRST CONTACT: *THE HMS RESOLUTION AND DISCOVERY LAND AT KEALAKEKUA BAY.*

SANDWICH ISLANDERS PLAYING IN THE SURF

SANDWICH ISLANDERS PLAYING IN THE SURF.

Lith of Endicott. N.Y.

"HE WAS CARRIED ALONG AT THE SAME SWIFT RATE AS THE WAVE, TILL IT LANDED HIM UPON THE BEACH. THEN HE WENT IN SEARCH OF ANOTHER SWELL. I COULD NOT HELP CONCLUDING THAT THIS MAN FELT THE MOST SUPREME PLEASURE WHILE HE WAS DRIVING ON SO FAST AND SO SMOOTHLY BY THE SEA."

—William Anderson, *Resolution* surgeon, 1777, about a surfer at Matavai Bay, Tahiti

THE ALTOGETHER ASTONISHING SURFER

Lieutenant James King, a member of Captain Cook's *Resolution* crew, wrote a detailed journal entry on boardriding. Recalling an afternoon spent on the beach at Kealakekua Bay, on the Big Island, King spoke of the surf zone's "prodigious violence," the "great violence" that seemed to befall a surfer being caught in a breaking wave, and the "great horror" of watching an islander wipe out. "The [natives'] boldness and address . . . was altogether astonishing, and is scarcely to be credited." King's passage set the tone for those looking to write about surfing in the eighteenth and nineteenth centuries. Of the few dozen descriptions of the sport during this period—most no longer than two or three paragraphs, written mostly by British and American explorers, merchants, missionaries, and wealthy adventure-seekers— mild bombast and polite disbelief were the rule.

There was some confusion, too, starting with the name of the craft itself. Hawaiians referred to it as *papa he'e nalu*, or "board for wave-sliding." English-speakers at first tried "floatboard," "sharkboard," "broad-board," and "bathing-board," with "surf-board" first used sometime in the 1790s. The terms "surfer" and "surfing" didn't take until the early twentieth century, replacing "surf-swimming," "surf-boarding," "surf-bathing," "surf play," and "surf sport."

A LATE-NINETEENTH-CENTURY HAWAIIAN SURFER.

SURFING IN DECLINE

After centuries of mid-Pacific isolation, the Hawaiian immune system was defenseless against the assorted germs, pathogens, and viruses brought by the first Westerners. Natives were cut down by cholera, typhoid, tuberculosis, measles, flu, mumps, small pox, scarlet fever, dengue fever, bubonic plague, leprosy, and venereal disease. At the time of Cook's arrival, an estimated four hundred thousand Hawaiians lived on the islands. By 1896 the number had been reduced to just over thirty thousand.

Hawaii was reshaped by more than these terrible new diseases. Native custom and culture were under attack as well, particularly with the arrival of American missionaries in 1819. Fewer than 160 Protestant missionaries lived in Hawaii, and none served in an official lawmaking capacity. But their influence on island policy and culture was so immediate and significant that islanders soon made reference to the "missionary monarchy." Protestantism briefly became the nation's religion, and a new code of missionary-backed laws and decrees were passed. Hula dancing was banned, as was the heavenly-scented flower lei necklace, which, as one missionary explained, could be worn in such a way among the natives as to have "a vicious meaning." Surfing itself was never made illegal, but it was tightly hemmed in by "blue laws" against gambling and nudity, both of which were nearly as important to the sport as riding itself. Take away the sex and wagering and all of sudden the whole thing was a lot less attractive to most natives. While Hawaii's missionary project operated at full strength for less than forty years, surfers would come to view missionaries with special contempt. The frock-coated clergyman was surfing's original authority figure. And that carries a lot of weight for a sport that has in large part defined itself through rebellion.

A HONOLULU-BASED AMERICAN MISSIONARY FAMILY, 1850.

EARLY REVIVAL

It's difficult to say just how weak surfing's pulse became in the 1800s. A report from 1852 says that the sport was "rapidly passing out of existence," and another from 1876 notes that surfing was "fast dying out." Other notices are less pessimistic. While the decline can't be accurately measured, the nineteenth century was without question a disaster for surfing. By 1890, however, the worst was over. The Hawaiian immune system had toughened up. The missionaries were long gone. The sport entered a quiet but sustaining period, almost a second incubation, that lasted just a few years. Despite few changes in technique, board design, or the number of participants, the sport and its practitioners reemerged looking different somehow—at least to the world at large. Surfing had been described by one of the original missionaries in 1820 as the pastime of "chattering savages," who represented "destitution, degradation, and barbarism." Not long after the dawn of the twentieth century, swashbuckling writer Jack London reintroduced surfing as nothing less than "a royal sport for the natural kings of earth."

A LATE-NINETEENTH-CENTURY WAIKIKI SURFER POSES WITH HIS ALAIA.

Chapter 2: Gliding Return, 1900–1945

REBORN

Surfing's revival in the early twentieth century had a lot to do with glamour and marketing. As wealthy American and European globetrotters scanned the world for suitably exotic getaways, their attention naturally gravitated to Hawaii, which was pulsatingly tropical and yet both English-speaking and American-run. Surfing—a "uniquely Hawaiian water sport," as it was often described—was a calling card like no other. Local governors, plantation owners, and hoteliers immediately recognized that island romance and excitement were uniquely distilled in the act of wave-riding, and surfing imagery was soon printed, stamped, embossed, and etched onto pretty much anything connected with the islands—from postcards and travel brochures to china tea cups and hotel wine glasses. The PR campaign worked. Surfing began a growth trajectory that, apart from a short-lived dip or two, has remained unbroken into the twenty-first century.

WOODCUTS LIKE THIS ONE BY CHARLES BARTLETT HELPED BRING SURFING TO THE ATTENTION OF THE REST OF THE WORLD.

HUI NALU CLUB

Class and wealth played a part in Waikiki's burgeoning surf scene. The Outrigger Canoe Club had two or three dozen hardcore surfers and canoeists, but its membership roll was filled with hundreds of wealthy surf dilettantes who mostly used the club for weekend brunching. In contrast, when a group of local Hawaiian surfers launched Hui Nalu ("Club of the Waves") in 1911, membership was small and talent-based. A sheltering *hau* tree in the middle of a beachfront vacant lot served as the Hui Nalu clubhouse, and the hotel next door allowed members to use its basement as a changing room. Hui Nalu and the Outrigger were located just a hundred yards apart from each other, and a mostly friendly rivalry developed between the two. Yet racial mistrust and class resentment wafted almost visibly across the beach between the *hau* tree and the Outrigger's terrace-bordered clubhouse and adjacent dance pavilion.

HUI NALU CLUB, 1915. FOUNDING MEMBER DUKE KAHANAMOKU IS SEATED IN THE FRONT ROW, FOURTH FROM THE RIGHT.

Wilhelm. Hilo Boyd. H. Coolle. D. Kahanamoku. Steamboat. H. Anahu.
Bishaw. N. Kahanamoku. Genoves. Holstien. Lewis. S. Kahanamoku. Leedo.
Liebtrey. Stubby Kruger. Duke P. Kahanamoku. H. Priest. A. Buckley. H. Awana.

JACK LONDON

American author and sportsman Jack London, not long after sailing into Honolulu in 1907, sat on a piece of beachfront grass next to the elegant new Beaux Arts-style Moana Hotel and watched "a majestic surf thundering in on the beach to one's feet." London lifted his gaze out to the lineup.

And suddenly, out there where a big smoker lifts skyward, rising like a sea-god out of the welter of spume and churning white, on the giddy, toppling, overhanging and downfalling, precarious crest appears the dark head of a man. Swiftly he rises through the rushing white. His black shoulders, his chest, his loins, his limbs—all is abruptly projected on one's vision. Where but the moment before was only the wide desolation and invincible roar, is now a man, erect, full-statured, not struggling frantically in that wild movement, not buried and crushed and buffeted by those mighty monsters, but standing above them all, calm and suburb.

London himself took to the surf, and after thrashing about ineffectively for most of an afternoon, he at last felt the "ecstatic bliss" of a long ride to the beach. His four-thousand-word essay on his Waikiki surfing experience, written longhand in a single morning's rush of enthusiasm and published as "A Royal Sport" in the October 1907 issue of the high-circulation *Women's Home Companion*, brought surfing to the public's attention like nothing before. The godfather of American he-man prose, London described waves as "bull-mouthed monsters" and his wipeouts were filled with "smashing blows." In his calmer moments, he also provided an excellent short course on the physics of a breaking wave, along with a primer on how to paddle through the surf zone, manage a wipeout, pick up an incoming swell, and guide a shoreward-bound surfboard.

JACK AND CHARMAIN LONDON, WAIKIKI, 1907.

GEORGE FREETH

In mid-1907, just a few weeks after meeting Jack London in Waikiki, a high-born part-Hawaiian surfer named George Freeth steamed out of Hawaii, bound for California. Freeth—quiet, sad-eyed, handsome, and one of Hawaii's best wave-riders—wouldn't be the first person to surf on the American mainland. But the surfing demonstrations he gave at Los Angeles-area beaches like Venice and Redondo provided a foundation for surfing in California. No surprise that surfing found a welcome home in Los Angeles. The city had already become an ideal place for the new and offbeat. In terms of surfing basics, it had sunny weather, beautiful beaches, tolerably warm water for most of the year, and consistent waves. Hundreds of miles of light-rail lines radiated out from downtown, with many lines terminating in newly incorporated beach cities. Just as important, Los Angeles would try anything; it inhaled people and exhaled ideas and trends. This was the only place in early-twentieth-century America where surfing might be embraced as something more than a curiosity.

GEORGE FREETH AND REDONDO BEACH PROTÉGÉS, AROUND 1909.

BEACHBOYS

While Freeth spread the wave-riding gospel in California, surfers in Waikiki gathered near the elegant beachfront verandahs of the Moana Hotel, and later the Royal Hawaiian. These surfers, informally vetted by hotel managers, were collectively known as "beachboys." They earned money by befriending tourists and serving in whatever capacity was required: island guide, surf instructor, lifeguard, babysitter, serenader, gigolo. It was an informal, tips-only business. Arrangements between beachboy and tourist, as frequent Waikiki visitor Cary Grant put it, were often based on "friendship, a handshake, and a bottle of scotch." Style counted for a lot. Beachboys wore the finest coconut-button, silk aloha shirts and the sharpest-creased pants in Waikiki. Money wasn't very important, except when it could be flaunted; more often than not, a beachboy on the receiving end of a "hundred-dollar handshake" from a grateful departing hotel guest would turn up at the bar that night and blow the better part of his windfall on a round for the house. Surfing was as important to these barefoot troubadours as their sexed-up, easygoing, empty-pocket deviancy. By combining the two, beachboys laid a foundation for what would later be called the surfing lifestyle.

WAIKIKI BEACHBOYS "SPLASH" LYONS (LEFT) AND "TOUGH BILL" KEAWEAMANI (BACK RIGHT) WITH AUSTRALIAN TOURISTS, LATE 1920s.

DUKE

Waikiki beachboy and Olympic gold medal swimmer Duke Kahanamoku was surfing's first and forever grand patriarch. He rose to fame almost in double vision— the esoteric wave-rider and the champion swimmer. His swimming achievements were towering, but they didn't define, or even redefine, the sport, which had roots in antiquity and a long, venerable list of champions. Surfing was a different story. After the 1912 Olympics, during his return passage from Stockholm, Kahanamoku began the ambassadorial work for which he is best known, giving surfing demonstrations on both sides of the American mainland. He later did the same in Australia and New Zealand.

Through his gracious example, surfing, while still exotic, was made accessible. He was so much at ease on a board that the ocean itself appeared less dangerous. It didn't hurt that Kahanamoku was tall and broad-shouldered, with high cheekbones, a radiant full-lipped smile, and a brushed-back crown of thick black hair— one admirer fairly described him as "the most magnificent human male God ever put on earth." Surfing would have caught on without Duke Kahanamoku, but not as quickly, and not with the same opening bolt of style and élan.

DUKE KAHANAMOKU, WAIKIKI.

EARLY SURFING IN AUSTRALIA

"Surf-shooting" on a board wasn't entirely new to Australia in 1914 when Duke Kahanamoku visited and gave demonstrations, but the Hawaiian gave the sport a stronger footing. Surfing more or less folded into Australia's "surf life-saving" movement, which spurred the formation of dozens of highly trained "surf clubs"—lifeguard militias, more or less—on popular beaches around the country. While still a junior member among English-speaking nations, Australia proudly took the worldwide lead in beach safety, and the bronzed clubbie, with his rubber swim cap and tiny pectoral-hugging swimsuit, became the country's first iconic figure. The Aussies would prove to be inventive with their wave-riding craft; the wave ski was developed here, as was the inflatable rubber Surfoplane, which later arrived in America and was renamed the "surf mat." In both countries, two or three generations of surfers got their first best waves on these soft, easy-riding, rectangular surf mats, which remained popular until the midseventies' introduction of the bodyboard.

MANLY BEACH SURF CLUB, SYDNEY, AROUND 1911; THIS CLUB WAS A FOUNDING MEMBER OF WHAT IS NOW CALLED SURF LIFE SAVING AUSTRALIA.

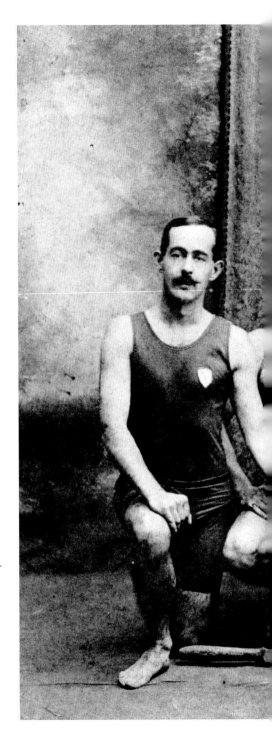

TOM BLAKE

Wisconsin-born Tom Blake was the first mainland American surfer to leave a mark on the sport. Within two years of his arrival in California, in 1921, he was one of the country's best all-around swimmers, and in 1924—now obsessed with surfing, although still a novice—he caught a steamer for Honolulu. Blake was a quiet, well-dressed man with tousled hair and a bulletproof jaw who didn't drink or smoke. He ate dry oatmeal straight from the bag, kept to himself, read a lot, and tinkered constantly. Surfboard weight, Blake thought, was a problem. He first tried drilling hundreds of holes through his solid redwood "plank" board, which he covered with wood veneer. Then he built the first rib-braced hollow board, getting the weight down to an airy 40 pounds. This new craft was tippy, hard to control, and vulnerable to any hole or crack. But newly-minted surfers loved its lightness, and California surfing's first real population spike, during the Depression, had much to do with the hollow surfboard. In 1935, Blake added a stabilizing fin to the back of his board. Prior to this, boards had been finless. While the surfer could steer, a little, by carefully leaning one way or the other, these boards were for the most part at the mercy of the wave. That all changed with the fin. "Never before had I experienced such control and stability," Blake later said, recalling his first wave using a finned board. Yet for reasons that can only be guessed at— the sport's innate reluctance to try new designs, maybe, or Blake's lack of popularity among Waikiki's surf gentry—the fin was mostly ignored for the next five years. Not until the early 1940s did it become a standard feature, and many of the best Hawaiian surfers continued using finless boards until the late 1940s.

TOM BLAKE POSES WITH HIS 14-FOOT "CIGAR" BOARD.

"I FOUND THE WATER GOOD, BETTER THAN THE LAND I WAS CUT OFF FROM. WATER SUPPORTS A REBEL, IF HE HAS THE WILL AND ABILITY TO SWIM."
—Tom Blake

TOM BLAKE, RIGHT, WAIKIKI.

Tom.

INCORPORATING VANITY FAIR

vogue

HOLIDAY TRAVEL
RESORT FASHIONS
DECEMBER 15, 1938
PRICE 35 CENTS

O © THE CONDÉ NAST PUBLICATIONS, INC

THE GLAMOUR OF SURF

In the 1920s and 1930s, surfing maintained its cultural image as a plaything for the rich and famous. A great many surfing newcomers were wealthy tourists vacationing in Waikiki. Duke Kahanamoku, throughout his long and mostly forgettable LA-based film career, often went to the beach to surf and socialize with his Hollywood cohorts. With four-color printing, surf photography further raised the sport's glamour level. Previously, black-and-white surf photos were sometimes hand-tinted, but now wave-riding appeared in all its multihued glory, with oceanic blues and greens, warm redwood-plank browns, and sharp color bursts from the new swimsuits. A glistening 1938 *Vogue* cover, shot from above, featured a beachboy in floral-pattern trunks and his red-headed tandem partner launching a ride at Waikiki.

VOGUE, *1938*.

MARY ANN HAWKINS

Surfing's gender gap narrowed during the 1930s—a tiny bit. The default setting for women beachgoers was to be ornamental rather than active, and those who counted themselves as "surfers" were often lightly bedewed tandem partners carefully steered through the lineup by proud boyfriends. Still, women found the new hollow surfboards easier to handle than the solid-wood planks. The latest swimsuits also helped, as they did away with the water-absorbing collars and leggings and pantaloons that had nearly dragged previous generations of American female surf-bathers to the ocean floor. For a handful of women, this was enough to get out there and ride. Mary Ann Hawkins, one of America's best junior division middle-distance swimmers, became the teenage queen of California surfing during the Depression. Hawkins won paddling events, rode alongside Duke Kahanamoku, stunt-doubled for *Bathing Beauty* star Esther Williams, hosted well-attended surfer soirees at her parents' house, and later married one of the state's best surfers, Bud Morrissey. A series of photographs in a 1938 issue of *Life* showed Hawkins walking smartly down the beach with her board, paddling out, and gliding back to shore with a radiant smile.

MARY ANN HAWKINS, PALOS VERDES COVE.

SURF CLUBS

Surf club membership wasn't mandatory for California surfers during the Depression, but by the end of the 1930s, you could have driven a Packard Super Eight from San Diego to Santa Cruz and had a hard time loading it up with nonaffiliated surfers. Unlike the surf-based organizations in Australia, California's clubs were focused on surfing, and a bit of paddling, and nothing else. California's best-known and best-organized group was the Palos Verdes Surf Club, founded in 1935 by a surfing dentist named John "Doc" Ball. Headquartered south of Los Angeles in Gardena, where Ball had a dental practice, the PVSC took its name from nearby Palos Verdes Peninsula, home to a quietly wealthy Mediterranean-themed bedroom community, as well as Palos Verdes Cove, a beautiful cliff-lined bay sometimes referred to as "Little Waikiki." New initiates pledged to conduct themselves "in a manner becoming a Club Member and a gentleman, so help me God." Meetings were held, minutes were kept, and the club schedule was filled with Saturday night banquets, fundraisers, and "socials." The surf club movement said a lot about how the sport was developing in America. Surfers now had the numbers and confidence to join together in organizations having little or nothing to do with extraneous things like lifeguarding or canoeing. Wave-riding was enough.

PALOS VERDES SURF CLUB GET-TOGETHER, LATE 1930s.

"GOOD SURFERS RODE WITH THEIR FEET CLOSE TOGETHER AND TRIED TO SQUARE OFF SO THAT THE HIPS AND CHEST WERE FACING SHOREWARD. THE BEST SURFERS DID A LOT OF PREENING. BICEPS WERE FLEXED. CHESTS WERE THROWN."

CALIFORNIA SURFER GENE "TARZAN" SMITH.

EARLY MAKAHA

In 1937, a teenage surfer from Waikiki named John Kelly invented a board called the "hot curl." It had a narrow rear end, a pointed nose, and the bottom surface near the tail was rounded, like a boat hull. Although finless, it had more "bite" than any board before it, and that was the point: Kelly wanted to ride bigger waves, and the first step toward that goal was to design a board with the necessary traction. The hot curl was it. Before the year was out, Kelly and a couple of his friends found themselves on a beach called Makaha, a lovely, arid, empty break on Oahu's West Side, where the waves broke from three-foot to thirty-plus. Within two or three years they were confidently paddling into waves bigger than anything they'd ever seen in Waikiki.

Other Waikiki surfers gave Makaha a try, but only a few made it a regular thing. "We'd lose guys in two ways," recalled Wally Froiseth, Kelly's buddy. "We'd drive out there, bragging the whole way about the big surf, and it would be totally flat. And they'd say, 'Ah, you guys are bullshitting,' and we'd turn around and drive back. The other thing that happened was, the surf would be so goddamn big they'd just sit on the beach, scared shitless, and not go out at all. Same thing. They couldn't wait to get back to Waikiki." Still, from that moment, Makaha was surfing's big-wave epicenter until the late fifties.

WOODY BROWN, BOTTOM RIGHT, AT MAKAHA.

SAN ONOFRE

San Onofre was the sweet and easy low-simmering crucible of American surfing in the 1930s and early 1940s. Tiny pod-like surfing communities took root from San Francisco to Virginia Beach to Miami and beyond, but San Onofre, located halfway between Los Angeles and San Diego, was where the mainland version of the sport shone brightest. The San Onofre surf was soft and long, almost perfectly engineered to work with a 50-pound wooden surfboard. It was the beach life, though, that gave the place a warm glow. Cut off from the highway, and totally undeveloped, "Sano" was a ragtag community unto itself. No lifeguards. No performing on behalf of tourists or reporters. No club rules to obey. A palm-frond hut was built in front of the dirt parking lot. Clams, halibut, bass, and abalone were brought up, cleaned and filleted, dumped into a huge cook pot, and served to all by the bowlful. "My Little Grass Shack" was strummed on ukulele. Not counting food fights and the occasionally beery night out, the San Onofre gang didn't act especially defiant or unruly—that would be a job for 1950s, Eisenhower-era surfers. But they were the first to imbue the sport with the pride and knowingness of an exclusive secret society.

SAN ONOFRE BEACH PARTY.

John Kelly, Wally Froiseth, and a few others began making day trips to Oahu's North Shore in the late 1930s. This was a different world compared to Makaha. Everything about the West Side, including Makaha, was isolated. The North Shore was rural but not empty; small farms took up many of the lots on the inland side of the Kamehameha Highway, and a handful of modest wood-frame cottages were scattered along the beachfront, most of them weekend retreats for the Honolulu gentry.

The two surfing environments were, and are, different as well. As terrifying a big-wave break as Makaha becomes at times, its location—in the lee of Kaena Point, Oahu's fang-shaped western corner—is actually protected from much of the year's biggest surf and heaviest weather. The North Shore squares up directly with both incoming waves and storms, which means bigger waves, plenty of rain, and stronger, less predictable winds. Beginning in Haleiwa, the seven-mile North Shore wave zone is denser and more complex than any other like-sized area in the world, with breaks often shingling one on top of another. Particularly in the early years, it was overwhelming.

Sunset Beach was the first North Shore wave Kelly and Froiseth and the rest of the hot curl gang rode. They liked it well enough, and they were awed by the sheer number of breaks along the North Shore. Makaha, though, remained their favorite surf-travel destination. Chasing bigger waves was a thrill, but it was also time-consuming and intense; by focusing on one break—Makaha—instead of roaming the coast from Haleiwa to Sunset, the whole operation was a bit more grounded. The North Shore became their second choice; a place to check when the West Side surf was too small. That would change. The following generation of surfers would view the North Shore as nothing less than a big-wave mecca.

SUNSET BEACH, OAHU.

Surfers rode waves differently on the new hot curl boards, aiming to lock onto an angle parallel to the curl and shoot across until the wave backed down ("trimming," as it's now called). Angling translated directly into more speed, and each new hot curl design change was like adding another top-end gear to a car. Riding styles changed, too. Duke Kahanamoku and his plank-riding crew were partial to headstands and backward riding. The hot curlers came up with a different set of tricks. They still rode from the center of the board with their feet close together, touching if possible, as the previous generation did, but the new flourish was to arch the back while in midtrim, as if a basic upright stance just couldn't be maintained in the face of such heavy acceleration. When the wave slowed, the hot curler shuffled back a foot or so, stomped the tail, and made a pivoting direction change—nothing too sharp—then quickly moved forward to get the board planning again.

Staring in the late 1930s, at a break called Queen's, a bulldog-shaped teenager named Rabbit Kekai would get into trim, then arch with teenage insolence as the curl spilled over his knees and waist; near the end of a ride, just to put a little flare into his pullout, he'd run to the front of his board, crouch down, bury the nose, and lean bodily into the wave face, throwing the tail out and around like a huge wooden scythe. Paddling back out, he'd smile and yell "society turn" whenever he saw an older surfer guiding a plank through a slow, deliberate change of direction. Kekai kept planing his boards down smaller and thinner, eventually paddling on a stiletto-like craft measuring just 7 feet 6 inches—in calm water, a bigger surfer could stand on Kekai's board and pin it to the bottom.

RABBIT KEKAI ON HIS CHARACTERISTICALLY NARROW HOT CURL.

DEATH AT WAIMEA

On December 22, 1943, a thirty-one-
year-old pacifist named Woody Brown
drove across Oahu to the North Shore
with a gung-ho Honolulu high school
surfer named Dickie Cross. They came
across no other surfers. World War II
had emptied every beach from Waikiki
to Malibu to Bondi. Arriving at Sunset
Beach that afternoon, Brown and Cross
rushed out into what appeared to be ten-
or twelve-foot surf. They quickly realized
that it was much bigger—too big, in fact.
Without catching a wave, both surfers
turned around for a quick retreat to shore
and discovered that the outgoing current was too strong to paddle against.
Twenty minutes later they were a half
mile offshore, with all routes to the beach
shut off—and the surf was still building. The pair paddled three miles west to
Waimea Bay, where Cross made a dash for
shore, got swallowed by an enormous set
of waves, and drowned. It was now dusk,
and Brown, out of options, having lost his
own board in the same set of waves, swam
for shore himself. He got lucky. Fifteen
minutes later, tumbling forward naked
on a shorebreak wave—his trunks long
since ripped away—Brown was pulled to
safety by a group of soldiers. Cross's death,
and the unimaginable two-hour, lost-at-
sea horror show beforehand, became a
cornerstone for what the next generation
of big-wave surfers often called the "North
Shore voodoo."

CLOSEOUT SET AT WAIMEA.

Chapter 3: Malibu Swing, *1945–late 1950s*

SURFING GOES SOCAL

Before World War II, surfing lived in the reflected light of the tropics, with Duke Kahanamoku's noble, dark-eyed visage shining godlike from on high. Surfers and lifeguards were one and the same (in Australia), or close associates (in America), and the sport in general was lightly spritzed in heroism. After the war, surfing began its long march to the near and far corners of industry and media, and it became the cool new activity of choice for droves of revved-up, bushy-blond, suburban Southern California teenagers. It traveled with pandemic speed north to Santa Cruz, east to the Atlantic Seaboard, farther east to Biarritz and Newquay, and south to Lima, Rio, and Durban. Surfing had in fact already been introduced to many of these places. But the postwar style of surfing—the Southern California style, with trunks worn low on the hips, with an often-shouted litany of stoking new words and phrases, and with a fervor not just to ride waves but to be known as a wave-rider and to do so in a way that might piss off nonsurfers—*this* was new.

THE MALIBU "PIT," 1950.

POSTWAR SURFBOARD DESIGN

Joe Quigg was one of the Los Angeles-area boardmakers, along with Bob Simmons, Matt Kivlin, and Dale Velzy, who helped reconfigure surfboard design in the post-war years. In the summer of 1947, Quigg got a board request from Tommy Zahn, his best friend and a fellow navy veteran. Zahn had just started dating Darrilyn Zanuck, the tiny blond seventeen-year-old daughter of Twentieth Century Fox mogul Darryl Zanuck. Zahn asked Quigg to make a board small and light enough for Darrilyn to load by herself into the backseat of her new Chrysler Town & Country convertible and drive up to Malibu. A week later Quigg handed Zahn a 10-foot 2-inch, 40-pound redwood-and-balsa squaretail, lifted slightly on both ends and gently curved on the rail line from nose to tail, with egg-shaped rails. The whole idea was to make the learning process easier for a hundred-pound teenage girl; each feature was designed to make the board as forgiving as possible.

Zahn presented the board to Darrilyn, borrowed it and returned it, then borrowed it again, and again, and eventually didn't bother to give it back. Dave Rochlen, another easygoing Santa Monica surfer-vet, rode the board and liked it, too. So did thirty-four-year-old surf hero Pete Peterson. It was all a bit of a charade. When borrowed, the Darrilyn board, by unspoken protocol, had to be used in a kind of bluff, grinning, throwaway manner. It was okay to play around with your girlfriend's board on a slow afternoon, when the surf was blown out. Serious wave-riding, though—that was still done on bigger, heavier, man-sized equipment. Never mind that Zanuck's board—a prototype for what would become the "Malibu chip"—was clearly the board of the future.

When Zahn and Zanuck broke up the following year, ownership of the 10-foot 2-inch board became an issue. Darrilyn, remembered fondly by Quigg as "the first girl to buy a surfboard, stick it in the back of her car, and drive up and down the coast learning how to surf," finally had to break into Zahn's garage and steal her own board back.

BOB SIMMONS, MALIBU, LATE 1940s.

BOB SIMMONS SURFBOARD

The Simmons board came without logo, stamp, builder's signature, or decorative touch of any kind, and its craftsmanship was only passable. Next to the elegant multiwood laminated planks made a decade earlier by Pacific System Homes, or the sleek mahogany hollows made by Robert Mitchell Company, Simmons's boards looked raw, if not flat-out crude. The builder himself couldn't have cared less. Engineered speed was what mattered to Simmons—the rest was frippery. Crowing to his less-enlightened fellows on the beach, Simmons would introduce his latest model as a "hydrodynamic planning hull." In a more playful mood, he'd simply call it "my latest machine."

Did the boards actually work? That depended on who was riding. On a long, straight line, they were the fastest things in the water, and for a few dozen speed-obsessed Southern California surfers, during the late 1940s and early 1950s, Simmons was nothing less than a boardmaking messiah. But a Simmons board was as limiting in its own way as a rocket car tearing across the Bonneville Salt Flats. Maneuverability would soon be performance surfing's main goal, and better turning meant the surfer not only had to occasionally sink the board's tail into the water but ride closer to the curl in order to better tap the wave's power. Both ideas disgusted Simmons. Surfboards, he believed, were meant to ride as high out of the water as possible, and the speed-line he followed often put him twenty yards ahead of the curl. Soon, a younger crew of Los Angeles shapers would turn the design wheel in another direction.

SAN DIEGO SURFER AND A BOB SIMMONS "SLOT" BOARD, EARLY 1950s.

A surf break becomes famous when it can advance the cause faster than any other. Malibu wasn't the right spot for the twenties or thirties, but the break was made to order for the postwar progressives who wanted to ride on a higher, faster line and then to swoop up and down across that line. Simmons, Quigg, Kivlin—hot California shapers all made their boards with Malibu in mind. The new all-balsa "chip" boards were all launched at First Point. "Malibu was the test track," boardmaker Dale Velzy later recalled. "I'd paddle out and see a guy on one of my boards just buried in the curl, and I could watch and see how the board was working. 'Look at that rail, it's really biting in,' that kind of thing."

Just like at Waikiki and San Onofre, Malibu changed the sport on land as well as in the water. In many respects, Malibu was like San Onofre, but with better surf. Malibu was also just far enough removed from Southern California's suburban reach to make being there an unsupervised, semiprivate, easily accessed adventure. No lifeguards. No local police force; Malibu was decades away from incorporating as a city. Loose-fitting clothes, bouncy slang, pride in the sport's detachment from other sports (and the insolence that comes with that pride), a default wariness toward other surfers, brief public nudity and forms of mild social rebellion—much of the surfer stylebook was drafted at Malibu, beginning in 1945.

FIRST POINT, MALIBU, EARLY 1950s.

DEWEY WEBER

By the midfifties, the sport's performance standard was being set and reset almost month to month at Malibu, and the surfer doing the most to push things along was a flashy, half-pint, peroxide-blond high school wrestling star named Dewey Weber. By the time he finished his first year of high school, Weber was famous three times over—first as a pageboy-coiffed model for Buster Brown Shoes, then as a national yo-yo champion, then as an all-state wrestler. After getting his driver's license at age fifteen, Weber all but lived at Malibu during the summer months and was one of Dale Velzy's top test pilots. Like Matt Kivlin before him, Weber viewed beachgoers as an audience in want of entertainment. But where the smooth-surfing Kivlin got attention by riding the point like Sinatra finger-pop-ping his way through "Witchcraft," Weber pounded it out like Jerry Lee Lewis— hands and elbows chopping the air, feet blurred as he ran for the nose, stopped, and just as quickly backpedaled. He was also the first surfer to fully understand the value of costuming: his mother made him a pair of bright red surf trunks, and Weber himself bleached his shock of already-blond hair to a radiant yellow-white. When he was seventeen, and Velzy handed him a red board to match, Weber became the show. Surfers got out of the water to watch him ride, and he knew it. "People stood on the beach and pointed," Weber once said. "You could actually see them pointing."

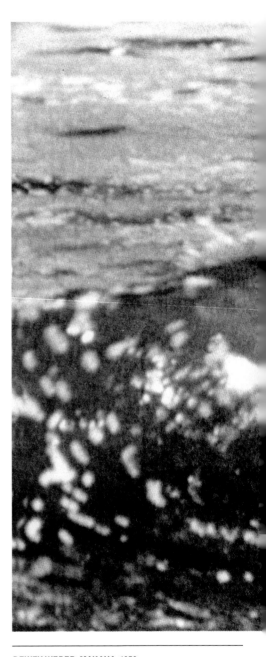

DEWEY WEBER, MAKAHA, 1959.

MAKAHA AND EARLY BIG-WAVE SURFING

In the early 1950s, several surfers decided to tackle big-wave riding as a kind of Manhattan Project, and the action took place mostly at Makaha. Surfers from Hawaii and California contributed equally to the new charge, but George Downing, a slender Waikiki regularfooter and the youngest of the group, went at it harder than anybody. Downing was twenty in 1950, but as the protégé to hot curl pioneer Wally Froiseth, he already had years of Makaha experience. He surfed with surpassing grace and brought a scholar's obsession to the sport: on calm days he snorkeled over reefs to better understand how they affected incoming waves, and he studied weather charts to better decipher swell creation. Downing took as much joy in riding waves as anybody. But he regarded the amount of surf-based knowledge left to be unearthed as both a challenge and a responsibility—almost a burden. Downing didn't take many days off. In 1950, he made himself a board he called the Rocket—a 10-foot, 35-pound, balsa-core beauty that would come to be regarded as the first great piece of specialized big-wave equipment. The Rocket was essentially a hot curl crossed with a Malibu chip. Downing kept the hot curl's streamlined shape, but he flattened out the back hull, knowing that a nonrounded surface would run faster through the water. Most importantly, he broke with hot curl orthodoxy and added a stabilizing fin. It was the only way, Downing realized, to attack really big waves. Made of balsa and redwood, with a resin coat that was fine-sanded and polished to a gleam, the Rocket looked fast just laying in the sand. Downing rode it for ten straight years. "I had so much confidence in that board," he later said, "that never once, if I got it trimming right, did I feel like I couldn't make it to the end of the curl line."

BUZZY TRENT, MAKAHA.

BUZZY TRENT

Buzzy Trent arrived in Hawaii in 1952 and never left. He was one of a small group of pioneering big-wave riders who made their way to Hawaii that included Greg Noll, Pat Curren, and Rick Grigg. Trent was a chatterbox and liked attention, and on a lazy afternoon among friends he'd hold court for hours, telling jokes and stories and making big sweeping gestures with his arms. Everybody laughed—but Trent was a little off somehow, as if all settings had been turned up to "10" and left there. Raw, ass-kicking masculinity came off him in waves. He had cinder-block arms and shoulders, a tiny *danseur* waist below a row of corrugated abs, and a smash-nosed face set low on a huge, blunt head. He trained constantly and could hold his breath underwater for three minutes. Trent viewed big-wave riding almost exclusively in terms of battle and combat. Boards were "guns," and while paddling out on a big day at Makaha, Trent would imagine himself as the Red Baron, banking through a hive of Allied planes. Downing, Froiseth, and a few others had built specialized equipment and pointedly gone out to ride oversized waves. But none of them saw the need to redefine themselves as surfers. They invented big-wave surfing; that was enough. It was Trent who formulated the grim, death-or-glory view of big-wave riding that would pass on virtually unchanged through the generations. It was Trent who invented the big-wave surfer.

BUZZY TRENT, SUNSET BEACH.

SURFING GOES INTERNATIONAL

In the 1950s, surfing slowly caught on around the world. Apart from Australia, the typical non-American surfing community was small and static, located on or near a resort beach, with a dozen or so lifeguards and weekenders all happily riding their outdated planks and hollows. Compared to the United States, surfers overseas tended to be older and more settled, and the sport was often taken up in an atmosphere of wealth and glamour. This was the case in both France and Peru. From the sand-bottomed lineup at Grande Plage, France's most popular break, surfers looked back to see the grand Hôtel du Palais and the beachfront Art Deco splendor of the Casino Barrière de Biarritz, where Edith Piaf and Yves Montand performed for elegant Galois-smoking *touristes*. Joël de Rosnay, France's first national surfing champion, wasn't the best surfer in the world, but as a teenage member of the Paris University ski team, surf instructor to Catherine Deneuve, and future PhD-holding director of applied research at the Pasteur Institute, he was without question the most debonair.

Surfing had meanwhile become a new recreational favorite among the Peruvian elite, falling in just behind polo and yachting, and taken up with great enthusiasm by the well-bred playboy sons of industrialists, bankers, plantation owners, military officers, and political attachés. In 1939, Carlos Dogny, the son of a French Army colonel and a Peruvian sugarcane heiress, built a modern split-level structure at the foot of the dusty brown beachfront cliffs in Lima and called it Club Waikiki. By the 1950s, a bowing white-jacketed attendant was on hand to wave club members into a lobby with marble floors and huge glass trophy cases. Cabana boys earning $300 a year ran down to a storage locker to fetch out $600 imported surfboards, to which they would apply a fresh coat of wax and then hand them off at water's edge. Queens and presidents were guests of honor at Club Waikiki's black-tie events. Membership was by nomination only, and the initiation fee was steep. "They'd paddle out and catch a wave, just to show they still had the old animal prowess," one visiting surfer said, describing the average Club Waikiki member. "Then a quick shower and lunch, followed by three or four cocktails on the terrace."

SURFING ON THE BASQUE COAST, 1963.

AUSTRALIA, 1956

In 1956, Australia hosted the International Surf Carnival as an adjunct to that year's Summer Olympics in Melbourne. California sent a twelve-man team, which included Los Angeles-area surfers Tommy Zahn and Greg Noll, both of whom brought their lightweight all-balsa Malibu chip surfboards. The Aussies themselves were still riding long, hollow, clumsy "toothpicks," which doubled as life-guard rescue boards, as they still mostly thought of surfing itself as a lifeguarding offshoot. The Aussies, as expected, dominated the carnival events. But for local surfers, the real action took place when the Americans waxed up their boards for a series of impromptu demonstrations. The first took place in thumping head-high waves at Sydney's Avalon Beach. Local boardmaker Gordon Woods was at work when the demonstration began. "This chap came running in, aghast," Woods recalled, "looked at me and said, 'You've gotta see these Yanks! They go *across* the

wave, turn around, and go back the other direction!'" Woods hustled down to the beach, saw it for himself, "and realized straight away that everything we'd accomplished up to that point was now redundant. That was it. The 16-foot boards were done overnight." Within forty-eight hours, Woods had arranged to buy one of the American-made boards—and he would go on to become one of the country's most successful boardmakers.

Once more, as with Duke Kahanamoku's introductory demonstrations in 1915, the course of Australian surf history had been charted by outsiders. It never happened again. Almost overnight, the sport began emancipating itself from the surf clubs and rescue work, and just ten years later Australia overtook Hawaii and Southern California to become the world's most progressive surfing region.

EARLY AUSTRALIAN SURFERS, 1940s.

BUD BROWNE AND THE FIRST SURF MOVIE

In 1953, a quiet forty-one-year-old Los Angeles schoolteacher and surfer named Bud Browne, working loosely from a model created a few years earlier by ski filmmaker Warren Miller, made a forty-five-minute film called *Hawaiian Surfing Movies*. After stapling a few notices on beachfront lightpoles in Santa Monica, Browne hosted a sold-out, one-night-only, 65¢-admission showing at a local junior high school. *Hawaiian Surfing Movies* had just one more screening. There were no profits to speak of. Yet Browne nonetheless believed that surf filmmaking, given a full calendar of show dates, could afford him a modest living. He was right; profits were modest—almost nonexistent. Still, Browne enjoyed the moviemaking process—the travel and the freedom, as well as the production—and kept at it. Again copying Miller, he decided to release one movie a year, and for a few years, the market was all his.

By 1958 Browne had three competitors, all from Southern California: Greg Noll, who had started building surfboards commercially; future *Endless Summer* producer Bruce Brown; and John Severson, who would soon found *Surfer* magazine. Each filmmaker was a one-man production company, responsible for everything: shooting, editing, scoring, narrating, promotions, booking, and accounting. They all used the same model Bell & Howell 16mm camera and shot the same A-list surfers at the same locations. Each film cost about $5,000 to make, was a little over an hour long, and consisted mainly of a series of short action sequences focusing on a specific rider or break. No plot. A few quickie comedy sketches. Great bootlegged soundtrack music. Surf movies traveled from town to town, screening at the local high school auditorium, Elks Lodge, or community center. Firecrackers were lit and rolled across the floor to the next row of seats. Bottlecaps zipped through the air. High-decibel beer-belches rang out. Moviemaking art was not the point. The gathering was. Being in the audience, drunk and loud and rowdy beneath a lowering haze of cigarette smoke, not watching the film so much as bouncing off it—that's what the early surf movie experience was about.

BUD BROWNE, EDITING ON THE NORTH SHORE.

Greg Noll rode Sunset Beach for the first time in late 1954 as a visiting seventeen-year-old Southern California high school student and boardmaker, and over the next ten years, as the North Shore was steadily explored and mapped, he became the sport's big-wave icon. No one could mistake Noll for any other North Shore surfer: in his prime, he was six foot two and 225 pounds, and he wore black-and-white striped "jailhouse" jams. The surf media nicknamed him "the Bull," partly for his congenital stubbornness and partly for the hunkered-down bovine power squat he used while riding. Noll was friendly and funny by nature but belligerent while drunk, which was often, and he brawled his way through his late teens and twenties. In later years, Noll recalled his fights in the same easygoing and affectionate bar-room voice he used for sharing big-wave tales.

In 1954, Makaha, on Oahu's West Side, was still big-wave surfing's hot spot, and that's where Noll intended to surf during his visit. But that first trip to the North Shore was a revelation. Driving a battered '37 Plymouth pickup through Haleiwa, a pair of enormous black lace panties looped over the truck's antennae ("from a wonderful three-hundred-pound Samoan lady who was very nice to us"), Noll and three friends rolled slowly up Kam Highway, craning their heads as they shouted and pointed at various likely-looking breaks. They eventually pulled over to ride some eight-footers at Sunset Beach. Nobody else was out. They didn't see another surfer all afternoon. Noll was surprised during the weeks to come that his friends weren't dying to go back and try again. He shouldn't have been. The North Shore's abundance was still too much for most people. Taking in the entire spread of breaks from Haleiwa to Sunset Beach, on a sunny day with a fifteen-foot west swell running, was kind of like staring into the cosmos on a clear night—beautiful but overwhelming. Most people looked, and then looked away. Not Noll. He was still a raw teenager, but persistent and calculating, and his surf-world ambitions were growing by the month. Some part of him must have recognized that a guy looking to make a name for himself in the sport would be well advised to break away from Makaha, where an older and more experienced group of surfers had already dug in. Noll couldn't wait to get back to the North Shore.

GREG NOLL AT THE FINISH LINE, LIFEGUARD PADDLE RACE, 1956.

FIRST TIME AT WAIMEA

In the mid- and late-1950s, Oahu's North Shore replaced Makaha as surfing's big-wave epicenter. It became a favorite of visiting California surfers, who rented beachfront bungalows and stayed for weeks, even months, at a time. Yet Waimea Bay remained off-limits. By 1957, nobody had tried it since Dickie Cross had died there about fourteen years earlier. Waimea didn't break that often, but when it came alive, it was the biggest ridable-looking wave on the North Shore. It wasn't just big, but explosive—unlike Point Surf Makaha, which gave you a roll-in start, the Waimea wave banked off a steep-faced underwater ridge so that the crest lunged up and out, then fell into the trough to detonate like a small atomic device. This rushing near-vertical takeoff, more than anything, is what kept North Shore surfers on the beach at Waimea, watching instead of riding, through the midfifties.

On a November morning in 1957, Greg Noll led a handful of surfers into the Waimea lineup. The surf looked about fifteen or twenty feet—big, but nowhere near full capacity Waimea. Nobody remembers for sure who rode the first wave. Years later, it came to light that a quiet Long Beach lifeguard named Harry Schurch had gone out earlier that morning, alone, and caught a couple waves. (Schurch eventually claimed it for himself, but in a backhanded way. "On the scale of human events," he said in 2008, "I understood the significance of what I had done . . . not really that much!")

Noll and his friends mostly got annihilated that first day at Waimea; a few waves were made, but mostly it was one cartwheeling wipeout after another. On the other hand, nobody died or even got hurt. Understanding that a wipeout here was survivable—this was the day's real achievement. The Waimea voodoo remained, but it was no longer paralyzing.

MIKE STANGE (TOP) AND MICKEY MUNOZ RIDE WAIMEA FOR THE FIRST TIME, 1957.

Chapter 4: Boom Years—A Massive Swelling, *Late 1950s–1967*

GIDGET

Fifteen-year-old Kathy Kohner of Brentwood was five feet tall, weighed ninety-five pounds, and learned to surf at Malibu in the summer of 1956 by trading peanut butter sandwiches to local surfers for the use of whatever board was lying around. They nicknamed her "Gidget"—a mashup of "girl" and "midget." Back home, Kathy talked incessantly about her surfing experiences, and at one point she told her father—a Czech-born, Sorbonne-educated Jewish writer who fled Europe just prior to World War II—that she was going to write a book about it. Frederick Kohner smiled, heard a little bell go off in his head, and offered to write it for her. *Gidget* is a work of fiction, but just barely. It's told in the breathless first-person voice of sixteen-year-old Frances Lawrence, who describes a wave- and romance-filled summer at Malibu. Kohner hammered out a first draft in just six weeks—not because the effort was gratuitous or rushed, but because in his own way he'd become as enthusiastic about surfing and the beach life as Gidget herself. The language appealed to him (Kohner's ear for the speech patterns of adolescent girls was nearly as sharp as that fellow eastern European émigré Vladimir Nabokov, whose *Lolita* came out just a few months before *Gidget*), and unlike many postwar American adults, he wasn't put off by the idea that the modern teenager had so much freedom and money and leisure time.

And so it was that a gushing Malibu-obsessed tomboy escorted surfing to its permanent seat at the long table of American pop culture. *Gidget*, the book, came out in 1957, and two years later the movie version proved to be the starting bell for a nine-year surf boom that took the sport from a California-centric phenomenon to a national craze to a hot international export. As the public went nuts for the surfing life, the wave-riding population doubled, then doubled again, and again, and probably a fourth time. It wasn't all Gidget's doing. But this loud, young, hard-charging period in surf history is forever linked in the popular imagination to this barefoot ingenue with the funny nickname.

FREDERICK AND KATHY "GIDGET" KOHNER, 1957.

EARLY REBEL SURFERS

In the 1950s, America was fascinated like never before with its teenagers and everything about them: the new car-crazy mobility; the rock and roll; the sense of entitlement that came from growing up in a singular age of wealth, ease, and security. Much of this didn't sit well with older Americans who, having suffered through the Depression and fought two global wars, expected the modern youngster to be, if not appreciative, at least respectful. Instead, adults were apparently facing the spread of what J. Edgar Hoover called the "juvenile jungle." California—ready to pass New York as the most populous state—had been identified as "the America to come," and Southern California especially was viewed as a special beacon for the young and disaffected, filled with bikers and runaways. And surfers. The new breed of wave-riders created a whole new style around crappy cars, lots of bare skin, and endless hours on the beach. "Things had changed since the era of the Palos Verdes Surf Club," Greg Noll later summarized, "when the guys were polite and behaved like gentleman. Now we just wanted to raise hell. And it wasn't a gradual change. It was like someone threw a switch, and all of a sudden we didn't give a shit about society or what other people thought of us."

PAT CURREN (RIGHT), YOKOHAMA BAY, OAHU.

HOBIE ALTER AND DALE VELZY

A Laguna Beach surfer named Hobie Alter had been making boards in his family's garage for a year or so when, in 1954, he bought a weedy vacant lot off the Pacific Coast Highway in Dana Point and began work on what would become the first full-service surfboard shop. Dale Velzy, Alter's main competition, opened a shop right down the road. Customers lined up behind one boardmaker or the other, giving their allegiance not just to a brand but to a form of surfing leadership. Alter, the younger of the two, was earnest and respectable, and his shop was as clean as Alter himself was clean-cut. Velzy smoked cigars, wore a huge diamond pinky ring, and kept a fat roll of hundred-dollar bills in his back pocket. In 1957, to celebrate a big sales year, Velzy paid cash for a 300 SL Mercedes; pulling up in front of his San Clemente shop, he'd pop open the gullwing door and walk toward the factory jingling the keys in one hand and holding a half pint of bourbon in the other.

Their salesmanship styles differed, too. In a bit of ad copy, Alter described his boards as having "evolved through careful and original changes, using proven principles and vast experience." Velzy, as even his most loyal followers would admit, was a hustler. He'd sidle up to a mink-coat-wearing divorcée looking to buy a board for her teenage son, touch her elbow, lean close, lower his voice, and say, "This here's a good-riding son of a bitch, ma'am."

Other boardmakers got into the game, but into the late fifties, Velzy and Hobie remained the two who really mattered. Velzy was the better craftsman, and charismatic enough to make his rivals seem all but invisible. But Alter had by far the better head for business. In 1960, when Velzy went down in flames for unpaid taxes, Hobie went from strength to strength and dominated the market for years to come.

HOBIE ALTER, LAGUNA BEACH, 1952.

FOAM BOARDS AND WETSUITS

The polyurethane foam blank was brought to market in the late 1950s, and the post-*Gidget* surf boom would be floated on boards made of foam, not balsa. For surfers, polyurethane was a modern wonder. The surfing wetsuit—the second big postwar breakthrough in surf equipment—was a godsend. San Francisco's Jack O'Neill didn't invent the wetsuit, but from the late fifties forward, time and again, he proved himself a masterful surf-world innovator and marketer. O'Neill stamped the company logo on a bright yellow hot-air balloon, and at big surfing competitions he'd land it majestically on a nearby beach. He famously ran a color ad showing a barebreasted model demurely pulling on an O'Neill short john, and he disarmed most critics by pairing the shot with surfing's first and last perfect slogan: "It's Always Summer on the Inside." In 1970, O'Neill introduced the one-piece fullsuit, which covered everything but the surfer's feet, hands, and head, a huge improvement over the old two-piece "layered" outfit. Corporate advantage was found even when O'Neill lost an eye in a surfing accident—as his bearded and eye-patched Long John Silver face was rendered into a company logo.

REDONDO BEACH SURFER WEARING A BEAVERTAIL JACKET.

THE SURF SHOP HAD LINOLEUM OR CHEAP CAR-
PET FLOORS AND FADED SURF-MOVIE HANDBILLS
TAPED TO THE FRONT WINDOW. IT WAS LOCATED IN
A SMALL, BARELY-REGULATED BUSINESS DISTRICT..
IT SMELLED LIKE RESIN AND NEOPRENE. YES, IT
WAS A RETAIL OUTLET. BUT IT HAD TO FUNCTION
AS A CLUBHOUSE AND SALON AS WELL.

EARLY SURF FASHION

Surfers, as a rule, don't wear much, but what they wear has to be distinctive. Clothes announce the fact that the wearer not only rides waves but represents a distinct species of beachgoer. By this definition, surfwear was invented on a lazy Southern California afternoon four or five years after D-Day, when members of the Manhattan Beach Surf Club—including boardmaker Dale Velzy, lifeguard Barney Briggs, and paddleboard champion Bob Hogan—handed around a pair of scissors so that each surfer could trim the length of the sailor pants they'd recently taken to wearing. Eighteen inches was removed, give or take, so that the frayed material ended just below the knees; sailor whites were the preferred color, but some club members went for blue. Either way, the pants cost just two-bits a pair at the local army-navy store—which was fortunate, as the thin material wasn't all that durable, and it was unstated club policy to steal and hide a fellow club member's shorts once they were hung out to dry. Having several pairs in reserve was a good idea.

LOS ANGELES–AREA SURFERS WEARING "NAVY CUT-OFFS," EARLY 1950s.

JOHN SEVERSON
AND SURFER

The first issue of *Surfer* magazine—a rough little thirty-six-page, black-and-white booklet made as a surf-movie promo piece—was put together by San Clemente surfer John Severson in late 1959. Severson was the right man for the job. He'd been surfing for half of his twenty-five years, and he was among the best all-arounders in the sport. Furthermore, he'd been documenting his experience since the beginning, first with his Brownie camera, then with cartoons, woodblock prints, and paintings. He also played trumpet, formed a barbershop quartet, and pitched for his high school baseball team. He had a masters in art education from Long Beach State. As fanatic a wave-rider as ever came down the pike, Severson, unlike most of his peers, didn't let the sport crab the rest of his life.

Looking back, the creation of the surf-mag trade in the 1960s seems not so much dramatic as inevitable; it filled an obvious and growing void. There was some risk involved—the morbidity rate for magazine startups has always been high. Then again, full-house crowds at surf-movie screenings up and down the coast proved there was demand for surf-related entertainment, and the small but growing number of commercial boardmakers could no doubt provide a magazine-supporting ad-revenue base. The first issue of *Surfer* looked like a scruffy but earnest art school project, beginning with its horizontal format, grainy cover shot, and hand-lettered logotype. The design was raw, even by that day's standard. But like the surf films of the period, polish didn't much matter. Severson's booklet was friendly, authentic, and handcrafted. Anything more sophisticated would have been out of synch with what was happening on the beaches, in the surf shops, and at the high school auditoriums where surf movies were playing. Severson hit a chord. And *Surfer*, by the following year, was an institution in the making.

SURFER *MAGAZINE*, 1962.

THE SURFER BI-MONTHLY

A John Severson Production

75¢

VOL. 3 NO. 2   MAY - JUNE

THE INTERNATIONAL SURFING MAGAZINE

PAUL GEBAUER • SUNSET BEACH, HAWAII

Surfing competition grew by leaps and bounds in the late fifties and early sixties, partly because it made the sport less strange for a lot of people. A newspaper editor could now turn a surfing article over to a sportswriter, who in turn arrived at a contest, saw the trophies and heat draw, and was immediately on familiar ground. The surf press (*Surfer* included), concerned about the sport's declining public image, saw that contests gave the sport opportunities to present itself as good and trustworthy. The beachfront city councils who sanctioned the events, meanwhile, did so in hopes of gaining some control over a group that increasingly seemed to feel entitled to its various social transgressions. Hot-rodders, after all, had been lured off the streets to participate in National Hot Rod Association–sponsored drag strip events, thus converting a societal menace into a weekend sport. Maybe it could work with surfers, too.

Yet the relationship between surfing and competition was awkward, for reasons Tom Blake had cited several decades earlier. "On one occasion, about 1918," Blake wrote in *Hawaiian Surfriders*, "a riding contest was held, the winner being judged on form, etc. Everybody disagreed and that led them to believe surfriding contests were impracticable." The awkwardness has never entirely gone away. Judging surfing is always difficult. The ocean often doesn't cooperate. The action, at best, is sporadic.

Still, by 1962, international surf contests were established in California, Hawaii, and Peru, and Australia was ready to get involved in a big way. Most competitions were decidedly lo-fi affairs, involving a card table, some folding chairs, an airhorn, a few pens and clipboards, and a bulletin board. Bunting and a PA system signified a big event. Judges were often barefoot and shirtless; makeshift judging towers were built with scaffolding planks and two ladders. If it wasn't a sunny beach day, the spectators might number less than twenty-five and be made up exclusively of competitors' friends, family members, and love interests. For a small but dedicated percentage of surfers, though, the desire to compete burned strongly, and competition thrived in years to come.

UNITED STATES SURFBOARD CHAMPIONSHIPS, HUNTINGTON BEACH.

HUNTINGTON BEACH

By the late 1950s, California's Huntington Beach was no longer the grubby oil boom-town it had been between the wars—with wooden derricks foresting the beachfront, tent cities, and roughnecks brawling in front of Main Street speakeasies just up from the Pacific Coast Highway. It wasn't Malibu, either. Atomized raw crude still scented the air, the beach was speckled with tarballs, and backyard oil pumps rhythmically nosed the ground at many of the cheap single-family cottages that covered the beachfront. Waikiki, Malibu, Palos Verdes, and Australia's Kirra Point— all had surf breaks lovely enough to be on postcards. Huntington was flat, poor, and industrialized. Soon enough it picked up another nickname: "Surf Ghetto."

Huntington's surfing pedigree, though, was first-rate. Hawaiian transplant George Freeth likely rode Huntington as early as 1907, and Duke Kahanamoku stopped by once or twice during the 1920s, by which time first-generation Huntington lifeguards were riding their planks on either side of the long munici-pal "pleasure pier." In 1959, the first West Coast Surfing Championships were held at Huntington, and as far as being a focal point for competitive surfing, the city never looked back.

UNITED STATES SURFING CHAMPIONSHIPS, HUNTINGTON BEACH.

MICKEY DORA

Beginning in the late fifties, Mickey Dora of Los Angeles surfed his way to the top of the high-performance pantheon with jazz-influenced grace and style, while also crafting himself into the sport's first and greatest antihero. Black-haired and handsome, with a flashing gap-toothed Bowery Boys grin, Dora looked the part of the rebellious surfer even before he fully embraced the role. He was a firecracker-lighting prankster and a gifted party crasher who kept a tuxedo in the trunk of his car for quick-change makeovers that got him into some of Hollywood's most exclusive black-tie events. On the beach at Malibu—his favorite break—or in the banquet room, Dora was a smart and witty conversationalist, cynical and entertaining, with expressive long-fingered hands that often floated up in vaguely Continental gestures.

Dora held jobs briefly and intermittently in his early twenties, but surfing took over his life to a degree that was incompatible with any work schedule. He existed for the most part on handouts from friends and supporters. He also shoplifted and stole from his employers, shook down awestruck young surfers, and convinced surfboard manufacturers to give him an endless supply of free "team rider" boards, which he used a few times and then sold. (Dora stepped up the criminal activities in his thirties, and eventually served time for felony check-writing and credit card fraud, as well as violating probation.)

Dora had his detractors, even during his Malibu glory years. But most surfers admired him, some to the point of zealotry, believing that Dora lied, stole, and scammed because that was the only way a genuine surfing purist could get by. Even those who regarded Dora as little more than a charismatic sociopath felt a kinship with him. Few played the rebel with Dora's commitment, but nearly all surfers embraced the concept and lived the part in smaller ways. Maybe they'd never commit felonies in the name of wave-riding. But for a few extra hours in the surf, they'd ditch class or leave work early; or lie to their parents, their boss, their wife; or speed through red lights just to get to the beach two minutes quicker. Dora's transgressions were everyone's, writ large. By championing him, surfers championed themselves

MICKEY DORA, MALIBU.

SURF CULTURE
GOES MAINSTREAM

Surfing had generated a lot of momentum by 1959—new boards, wetsuits, competitions, surfer-produced films, a magazine on the way—and the sport was at a tipping point. Then *Gidget*, the Columbia Pictures' movie, was released in April of that year and pushed surfing over the top. A nine-year surf explosion followed. While wave-riding itself became more popular, the boom was mostly a cultural phenomenon, one that spread into the near and far reaches of teenage consumerism. Tens of thousands of young people slow-danced to "Surfer Girl" and thronged the local Bijou to see *Beach Blanket Bingo* and *Ride the Wild Surf.* They took their shoes off and did the Surfer Stomp to Dick Dale records. They shopped at May Company and bought nylon competition-stripe trunks from the McGregor Surfer Collection, Hang Ten sneakers, and Cutex "Wipe Out Pink" toenail polish. *Cosmo* and *Playboy* ran surf fashion layouts. You expected Coppertone and Jantzen to roll out surf-theme ad campaigns, but that was just the start. A ubiquitous Hamm's Beer billboard showed hot California surfer Rusty Miller jamming down the face at Sunset Beach. Pepsi did surf ads. So did Triumph, Mobile, Chevy, and Dewar's. It didn't matter if you were a few state lines removed from the coast; the boom was inescapable. As the *Saturday Evening Post* put it in 1967, surfing was "the most successful California export since the orange."

The beach fashion hook, in particular, was set deeply into the minds and wallets of consumers. The new styles were loose, comfortable, and inexpensive, and the Western world was steadily if incrementally moving toward a more casual dress style—with JFK doing his part over family weekends at Hyannis Port, in his black-frame Wayfarer sunglasses (same as the Malibu guys) and his loose shirttail flapping in the warm Atlantic breeze. Surf music and beach movies would vanish at the end of the boom and never again have the same cultural presence. Surfwear fell out of style, too, but only temporarily. More booms were coming, and they'd be fueled start to finish by surfing's fashion houses.

ANNETTE FUNICELLO AND FRANKIE AVALON IN BEACH PARTY.

PHIL EDWARDS WAS THE MOST RESPECTED MAN IN THE SPORT DURING THE LATE FIFTIES AND EARLY SIXTIES. HE INVENTED POWER SURFING, AND HE WAS SOMEHOW BOTH ROUGH AND ELEGANT. EDWARDS WOULD GO INTO A TURN LOOKING AS IF HE'D BEEN SHOVED, THEN FINISH OFF SMOOTHER THAN GENE KELLY.

PHIL EDWARDS, TRESTLES.

THE PUBLIC IMAGE

East Coast journalists were the first to publicly laugh at surfers. By the midsixties, the sport had jumped across to the Atlantic Seaboard and was thriving on beaches from Florida to New England, but it was still viewed as a quintessential Southern California product—making it kooky almost by definition. While surfers had often done their best to present surfing as rebellious and eccentric, it was a matter of interpretation as to whether the results were cool, sexy, stupid, dangerous, or some combination thereof. For establishment writers, in any event, stepping on the sport was a casual way to reassert the East Coast's metropolitan superiority. New York writer Gilbert Rogin, for his 1965 *Sports Illustrated* surfing feature on teenage world champion Joyce Hoffman, seemed to go out of his way in serving up quotes by Hoffman that made her and the sport look ridiculous.

Halfway through the article, Rogin suddenly detours for an interview with North Shore big-wave heavy Fred Van Dyke, who mused on the hidden motives of those who paddle out into huge surf. "It's absolute terror. Big-wave riders are scared people . . . they have to go out there to prove they're not afraid, to prove their masculinity." Van Dyke was just warming up. "Most big-wave riders," he concluded, "are latent homosexuals." Van Dyke spent years explaining that he didn't mean queer homosexuals, but the Freudian kind, where guys want to do guys-only stuff—like surf—and only care about what other guys think of them. All perfectly true. Nobody was listening, though. Van Dyke wore the quote around his neck for the rest of his life.

And so it went throughout the sixties surf boom, and after. Athlete, adventurer, gigolo, hoodlum, dimwit—in terms of public image, the surfer could be seen in nearly any way that suited the viewer.

FRED VAN DYKE (LEFT), SUNSET BEACH.

THE

SURFING WORLD

MONTHLY

AUSTRALIA'S SURFING MAGAZINE

75 CENTS CN.

VOL.1 NO.4

Registered at the General Post Office, Sydney, for transmission by post as a Periodical.

COMPLETE WORLD TITLE COVERAGE

MIDGET FARRELLY

By the early sixties, surfing in Australia had at last removed itself from the shadow of beach lifeguarding. For a while, Aussie wave-riders were content to draft along behind the Californians. That changed when a buttoned-down teenager from Sydney named Midget Farrelly moved into the international ranks. Farrelly was an atypical Australian champion. He was bright and at times wickedly funny, but he never wallowed in Aussie mateship and all its attendant vices. He spoke with a vaguely upper-class British accent and was prone to lecture other surfers on their responsibility to the sport's public image. Farrelly became a surf hero in Australia when he won the Makaha International Championships in 1962, thus bringing the most prestigious title in surfing home to a grateful sports-crazed nation. He was just eighteen and didn't yet look old enough to shave. No surfer alive, though, could match Farrelly for resolve and diligence. For instance, as a young teen, Farrelly determined that Phil Edwards was the world's best surfer, an appraisal many shared, and he became a student from afar. He mastered the better part of Edwards's gestures and body language, except where the older California surfer was spontaneous and quirky, Farrelly was precise, calculating, and hypnotically smooth.

In May 1964, the first World Surfing Championships were held over a single weekend at Sydney's Bondi Beach. Perfect weather, adequate waves, and many of the world's best surfers in attendance. In the final, Farrelly kept up with the leaders, got a buzzer-beating wave at the end for a near-perfect score, and took the title. Not long after that, Australian surfing itself became the sport's progressive epicenter.

MIDGET FARRELLY ON A SURFING WORLD *COVER DEVOTED TO THE 1964 CHAMPIONSHIPS.*

Based on demographics alone, the post-*Gidget* boom exploded loudest on the American East Coast. In 1959, there were less than 250 dedicated riders between Miami and Cape Cod. By 1966, the East and West Coast surfing populations were nearly equal, at about 200,000 each. More than ten thousand spectators attended that year's East Coast Surfing Championships, and Hobie Surfboards shipped seven out of every ten boards to its Atlantic Seaboard dealers. During this period, Southern California was Rome to the sport's growing worldwide empire, but nowhere were communications so direct, supply lines so open, the surf-citizenry so devoted as the East Coast. Kids might prefer California brands—Hobie, Jacobs, Weber, *Surfer*, Katin trunks, O'Neill wetsuits—but local surf entrepreneurs rushed in with homegrown items to service a market that was growing by the week: Ron Jon Surf Shop in New Jersey and Hannon Surfboards in New York; *Atlantic Surf* and *Surfing East* magazines. It didn't hurt retailers that locals had more time to shop, since East Coast surf, for a variety of oceanographic reasons, is smaller, weaker, and less consistent than it is on the West Coast.

By the midsixties, the hottest surf action on the East Coast was taking place in central Florida, on a long, thin, humid, suburban-lined ribbon of beach-break peaks between Daytona Beach and Melbourne. On this stretch, the hottest gun was a teenage fireplug named Gary Propper. At the 1966 East Coast Surfing Championships, Propper hotdogged his way past visiting surf icon Dewey Weber to take first place. On land, he talked constantly, hustled and promoted—"Yes, I'm Gary Propper" read the front of his T-shirt—flashed his wide cherubic smile for the cameras, and lost his temper on a dime.

Propper became the voice of East Coast regional pride. The East Coaster, he wrote, should be "stoked to say they're from Cocoa Beach, or Belmar, or Long Island," and not have to "fake it and say he's from Hermosa or Santa Cruz. We can still be influenced. But people can also be influenced and impressed by us." Future generations of East Coasters would accept this idea as their surfing birthright, until the day finally arrived when East Coast surfers were not only influencing and impressing the surf world but dominating it.

GARY PROPPER, COCOA BEACH, 1967.

MIDSIXTIES AD SHOOT FOR HANG TEN BEACHWEAR.

COSMO, PLAYBOY, SPORTS ILLUSTRATED . . .
MAGAZINE PUBLISHERS LOVED TO RUN SURF
FASHION LAYOUTS. THE CLOTHES WERE NEW AND
HIP. BETTER STILL WERE ALL THOSE YOUNG, SLIM,
CALIFORNIA-TANNED LEGS, ARMS, SHOULDERS,
BACKS, AND STOMACHS. THE BEACH FASHION
HOOK WAS SET PERMANENTLY INTO THE MINDS
AND WALLETS OF AMERICAN CONSUMERS.

WOMEN SURFERS

Two-time world champion Joyce Hoffman of Capo Beach was blond and attractive, with a radiant smile and the deadliest competitive drive in all of surfing during the 1960s. "My idea of having fun," she once said, "is being the best at something and winning all the time." *Seventeen*, *Vogue*, and *Teen* all ran profiles on her. Triumph gave her a free TR4 roadster and used her in ads. She was Miss Capistrano Beach and named by the *Los Angeles Times* in 1966 as Woman of the Year. As the *Times* reported, Hoffman was a straight-A student who didn't smoke or drink, liked Andy Williams records, and preferred (in Hoffman's words), "nice, clean movies . . . not the new trash they're putting out." There was eye-rolling among surfers at Hoffman's sanitized presentation of herself and the sport, but nobody gainsaid the fact that she was a kick-ass surfer who made a big impression on middle America.

Female celebrity and empowerment in the sport, though, was exceedingly rare. Women were more often treated as decorative: rubbing up against a male surfer in an advertisement, handing out trophies at the awards ceremony, or just watching the valuables while the guys hit the waves. Surf movies included plenty of girls, but most films didn't have a single clip of a woman wave-riding. This was surfing sexism during the boom age. It only got worse in years to come.

JOYCE HOFFMAN, 1966 WORLD CHAMPIONSHIPS, SAN DIEGO.

BEACH BUNNY AND SURFER GIRL, SYDNEY, 1966.

FOR FEMALE SURFERS, ATTENTION OF ANY KIND WAS THE EXCEPTION. WOMEN SURFERS—NOT BEACH GIRLS AND BIKINI MODELS, BUT ACTUAL SURFERS—WERE MOSTLY IGNORED AND OVER-LOOKED. *SURFER* MAGAZINE'S COVERAGE OF THE 1965 WORLD CHAMPIONSHIPS RAN TO EIGHT TEXT-HEAVY PAGES. TWENTY WORDS, TOTAL, WERE GIVEN TO THE WOMEN'S EVENT.

NUUHIWA AND NOSERIDING

DAVID NUUHIWA, 1966 US CHAMPIONSHIPS.

Noseriding—hanging five, hanging ten, hanging heels off the board's front end—was surfing's obsession, its "sport within a sport," in the midsixties, and Hawaiian-born David Nuuhiwa was the greatest noserider of the day. His talent was almost otherworldly, with one graceful turn linking to the next, his panther-like steps to the front of the board setting up long, time-suspending noserides. All that, plus Nuuhiwa was dark and quiet and handsome, with a Miles Davis level of cool. By early 1966, a few years after moving to California, he was all but levitating over the American surf scene with contest wins, magazine covers, and star turns in surf movies.

As Nuuhiwa changed surfing, it changed him. Wary and shy during his midteens, by eighteen he'd cultivated a cooler-than-thou imperiousness—and this, too, was something new in the sport, the celebrity surfer. To then, famous surfers (Mickey Dora excepted) had for the most part offered themselves to the media as good-natured beach jocks. Nuuhiwa wanted to be a surfing rock star. In 1966 he cut his thick black hair into a Mick Jagger–*Aftermath* shag, didn't return phone calls, and used the royalties from his hot-selling David Nuuhiwa Noserider signature board to buy a purple Porsche 911, which he drove like hell to Whisky a Go-Go on Sunset Strip. "For awhile," as one surf writer noted, "David was surfing itself, a pharaoh, noseriding to the adoring masses."

BRUCE BROWN AND THE ENDLESS SUMMER

Nothing better encapsulated the 1960s surf boom, nor more clearly marked its end, than *The Endless Summer*, Bruce Brown's cheerful crossover documentary hit. Filmed in 1963 at the very height of the boom, and made for just $50,000, *The Endless Summer* wasn't released to general audiences until fall 1966. Brown's premise was simple—follow two actual California surfers, Robert August and Mike Hynson, around the world in search of the perfect wave—and this resulted in an almost offhand casualness that captured a magical vision of the surfing life.

Endless Summer was Brown's sixth full-length work. While, in the movie, Brown himself came off as the very embodiment of California beach cool—blond, tan, and grinning, with, as writer Tom Wolfe described, a "Tom Sawyer little-boy roughneck look about him, like

Bobby Kennedy"—he was also a driven and meticulous filmmaker. *Endless Summer,* apart from being fun and joyous, was a perfectly controlled work. Critics loved it. The *New York Times* lauded its "hypnotic beauty and almost continuous excitement." *Time* called it "an epic." *Newsweek* named it as one of the year's ten best movies. But what *Endless Summer* reviewers didn't know, what movie-going audiences from Flagstaff to Rochester didn't know, was that the focus of their adoration had already disappeared. The movie played like a coda for a memorable period in the sport that, rather than being endless, vanished all too quickly. By mid-1967, surfing went into pupation, and it emerged months later, in a strobe-lit cloud of pot smoke, as a radically different sport.

SURFER *MAGAZINE* AD.

The Endless Summer

is coming
to a theater
near you !

Because of the tremendous enthusiasm for "The Endless Summer," we have enlarged it to 35mm. It can now be shown on big theater screens throughout the country. Watch for the New York City opening in June.

BRUCE BROWN FILMS

P.O. BOX 714S - DANA POINT - CALIFORNIA - GYpsy 69373

Chapter 5: Barefoot Revolution, 1966–1974

SHORTBOARD REVOLUTION

It has always seemed a bit grandiose to call any surfing era a "revolution," but the late-sixties shortboard revolution was just that—in miniature, at least. Old ways and ideas were thrown over in a furious rush. Young leaders ground their bare feet into the backs of their predecessors and pushed forward. Like most revolutions, it had an exciting, necessary, even righteous urgency that could, from other angles, also appear excessive, wasteful, and almost silly. Never before or since has the sport changed so much and so abruptly.

The shortboard revolution thundered across the surfing landscape for roughly three years, beginning in 1967. It was really two distinct but conjoined movements: one equipment-related, the other cultural.

During that period, surfboards went from being bulky 9-foot 6-inch, 26-pound noseriders to 6-foot 6-inch, 9-pound "mind machines." Surfers, meanwhile, virtually melted into the counterculture. "You were on the bus or off the bus," surfer journalist Drew Kampion wrote, looking back years later at the shortboard revolution. "You believed in gravity or you believed in space."

Lines between Us and Them were thus sharply drawn. A lot of bad vibes floated just behind the peace banners. No surprises there. Revolution, as Chairman Mao said, is not a dinner party.

SUNSET BEACH, 1969.

GEORGE GREENOUGH

George Greenough of Santa Barbara, a straw-haired, eccentric kneeboarder and design savant, was both source and inspiration for the equipment changes that marked the shortboard revolution. On a homemade, 7-pound, flex-tail kneeboard, with a long swept-back fin, Greenough, by 1966, was riding like a visitor from ten years in surfing's future. He cranked out bottom turns where his board tilted up almost 90 degrees, and his hip and thigh skimmed flat along the water surface. He effortlessly performed figure-eight cutbacks. Because his board was so small, and because his riding profile was so low, it was much easier for him to get inside the tube—until the early 1970s, he spent more time in what people called "the green room" than the top one hundred surfers in the world combined.

Much of Greenough's design work was done in Australia, which became a second home. He liked the energy Down Under. The Aussies, more so than the Americans, seemed to push a little harder and were more open to new ideas. California surfing, after two decades as the sport's dominate power, had become indolent and entitled. Even after Midget Farrelly of Sydney won the 1964 World Championships, few Americans accepted the fact that Australia was now another major surf-world player. Fewer still understood the momentum that had been building since then among Australia surfers and boardmakers. Greenough understood perfectly. The shortboard design seed was his to plant, and he chose to do so Down Under.

GEORGE GREENOUGH AT HONOLUA BAY.

SHORTBOARDS: BOB McTAVISH AND NAT YOUNG

Bob McTavish and Nat Young, both from Australia, were the surfers who took Greenough's kneeboard equipment and radical wave-riding approach and reconfigured them to work for stand-up surfers. The friendly, barrel-chested McTavish was equally talented as a surfer and boardmaker. Young made boards, too, but he was primarily a big, powerful, aggressive surfing genius. In 1966, Young and McTavish both were pushing what they called the "involvement" form of riding, where the idea was to turn the board up and down constantly around the curl, usually at the expense of noseriding. To that end, they made boards that were thinner and lighter than average, with a Greenough-designed swept-back fin. In September, Young flew to San Diego for the World Surfing Championships, where, as the reining Australian champion, he was angling for a showdown with noseriding prodigy David Nuuhiwa of California. The matchup was a bust, however, as Young powered his way easily to the winner's podium. Back in Australia a few months later, McTavish, looking to push the performance boundaries further, went smaller yet with his board and added a deep V-shaped profile to the underside of the board near the tail, to encourage sharper turning. He wrote "Plastic Machine" in huge psychedelic letters across the bottom.

By mid-1967 McTavish had dropped his board size down from just over 9 feet to 7 feet 6 inches (former world champ Midget Farrelly was doing much the same, working just down the beach from McTavish), and performance barriers were falling by the week. Nobody in California or Hawaii had any idea what the Aussies were up to. Furthermore, when McTavish debuted his V-bottom at Sunset Beach, Hawaii, at the end of the year, the big surf proved too much for the board's turning capabilities. But the seed was sown. Progressive surfers everywhere took McTavish's design and ran. Surfboards would continue changing at a head-spinning rate throughout 1968 and into 1969, and minds changed and expanded along with them.

BOB McTAVISH, SHORTBOARD REVOLUTIONARY.

"THE KID COULD DO ANYTHING!" BOB McTAVISH SAID OF NAT YOUNG. "HE'D PADDLE FASTER THAN WAS HUMANLY POSSIBLE, STOP, LET OUT A STRING OF OBSCENITIES, TAKE ANY WAVE HE WANTED, SWEAR AGAIN, LAUGH, PADDLE BACK OUT, SWEAR A FEW MORE TIMES, TAKE THE VERY NEXT WAVE. AND HE COULD DO IT ALL DAY." AS YOUNG HIMSELF PHRASED IT IN THE CUDGELING FIVE-WORD EPIGRAPH HE USED WHEN SIGNING AUTOGRAPHS: "NAT'S NAT AND THAT'S THAT."

NAT YOUNG, BYRON BAY, 1967.

SURF, DRUGS, AND
ROCK AND ROLL

In the late sixties, surfers ran, jumped, and cannonballed into the deep end of the counterculture. Surf magazines published free-verse poetry: "You are Moses / with a fiberglass snake / entering eternity." Revered boardmaker Dick Brewer put on a pair of surf trunks each morning, drove out to a tiny Buddhist temple in the hills of Kauai, sat in full lotus for an hour, then drove back to his workshop and fired up the planer. The sport began to groan beneath the weight of its own significance and meaning. "Because surfing, in its pure form, deals with an equilibrium involvement between man and his nature," surf journalist Drew Kampion wrote in 1970, "it becomes, almost by definition, an ecologically pure undertaking. Perhaps even an undertaking so basic that it performs an evolutionary function."

Fashion-wise, a lot of surfers took their dress cues from album covers and *Rolling Stone* magazine. Attendees at the 1969 *Surfer* Magazine Readers Poll Awards banquet wore beaded headbands, paisley-print scarves, fringed suede jackets, and half-tint wireframe glasses—the whole scene could have been transported straight from a backstage trailer at Woodstock.

Drugs, meanwhile, were cheap, available, and popular, and surfers availed themselves freely. Wilkin Surfboards in Los Angeles debuted its Meth Model in 1968 with the tagline "For Those Who Like Speed," and top surfers umbilically attached themselves to a giant ceramic hookah in *Morning of the Earth*, Australia's most popular early-seventies surf movie. For most surfers, as photographer Jeff Divine recalled, surfing wasn't just about surfing; the full experience involved "parking on the beach, smoking pot, taking acid, putting huge speakers on top of the car and blaring Santana, Hendrix, and the Doors." There were holdouts, including 1964 world champion Midget Farrelly and 1968 world champion Fred Hemmings. There were also dozens, hundreds, of drug casualties. But as one first-generation shortboarder put it, "The mood of the times made for a really creative period in surfing, and the mood was largely the result of getting stoned."

PACIFIC VIBRATIONS POSTER, 1970.

LATE-SIXTIES SURFERS LOVED HONOLUA BAY ON MAUI, BECAUSE THE WAVE WAS LONG, HOLLOW, AND FINELY TAPERED. ADVENTUROUS SURFERS MIGRATED FROM OAHU TO MAUI TO TAKE ADVANTAGE OF THE STILL-UNCROWDED HONOLUA LINEUP, DIRT-CHEAP RENT, AND THE WORLD'S BEST POT.

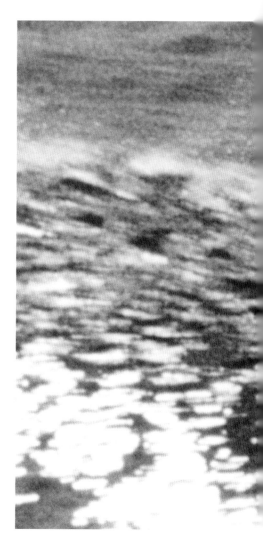

BARRY KANAIAUPUNI, HONOLUA BAY.

SURFER TUNES IN, TURNS ON

Surfer founder and publisher John Severson didn't just embrace the counterculture, he turned it into a sound business practice. In early 1968, *Surfer* remained the bulwark of surf media conservatism. The photography was first-rate, the magazine was well-organized and professionally assembled, and circulation was holding steady. It was also as predictable as oatmeal. Severson himself, meanwhile, had taken up golf, joined a country club, and bought a new Jaguar sedan, which he kept sand-free. His introduction to pot in early 1968 seemed to break his bourgeois fetters at a single blow. Before the year was

out, he'd gotten into the new shortboard trip, grown a luxuriant Sergeant Pepper's mustache, and remodeled his magazine. The turnaround was astonishing. Shimmering colors, free-form poetry, drug references, and stylized graphic elements pulled from *Rolling Stone, Esquire,* and *Graphis.* Ad revenue shot up. In 1970, *Communication Arts* magazine did a feature article on *Surfer* and gave the July issue an "Outstanding Cover Design" award.

SURFER *MAGAZINE, 1968. EDITOR STEVE PEZMAN (LEFT) AND THE* SURFER *STAFF.*

WAYNE LYNCH

Wayne Lynch of Australia was a rural-born fisherman's son, from a state—Victoria—that had never before produced an A-grade surfer. At age eleven, one year after he began riding waves, he entered and won an all-ages competition. At thirteen he won the first of six consecutive Victoria state juniors' titles; he also won four straight national junior division titles. But Lynch created excitement that had nothing to do with his contest record. What mattered were the incredible photos of him that trickled out of Australia in mid-1968. One of the shots, a grainy black-and-white taken at Bells Beach, was the photographic mindblower of the year: at the base of a six-foot wave, Lynch had his board jammed into a bottom turn so extreme that three-quarters of the board's bottom surface, and the entire fin save an inch at the very tip, was exposed. The move was advanced to the point of being incomprehensible, especially to the Americans, many of whom still thought hanging ten was the last word in performance surfing. What really made the photo was Lynch himself: poised and controlled, thin sixteen-year-old arms casually raised and bracketing his head, right hip jutting out to lead the turn—everything about his body position suggested that this maneuver wasn't accidental or experimental, but familiar. Other surfers, especially in Australia, were making great strides on the new short surfboards. Lynch alone made the quantum leap.

WAYNE LYNCH, BELLS BEACH, 1968.

LOCALISM

California surfing turned inward during the late sixties and became the birthplace of a more-muscular beachfront aggressiveness, soon to be known as localism. Most of it was simple turf-marking by resident surfers: spray-painted graffiti ("If you don't live here, don't surf here") or rubbing surf wax across the windows of a visiting surfer's car. Occasionally there were fistfights in the water or on the beach. At a Santa Cruz surf contest in 1969, under cover of night, local surfers pushed a judging scaffolding off a cliff into the ocean. In Palos Verdes, visiting surfers were pelted with rocks. For surfers, the thinking went: If the current sins of modern surfing—the now-crowded lineups and overhyped competitions, the boom that led to the rampant selling of the sport—had originated in California, then perhaps it was time to set things right. Or at least to safeguard the good that was left. Really it was just beachfront vigilantism. Still, localism traveled well, and by the early seventies it was spreading, and flourishing, in Hawaii and Australia.

TOP: LOCALISM OCCASIONALLY TURNED VIOLENT.

BOTTOM: SOUTHERN CALIFORNIA, 1973.

LOCALS ARE NOT RESPONSIBLE
FOR DAMAG TO DOWN-SOUTHERS CARS

SOUL SURFING

Surfing competitions fell out of favor during the shortboard revolution, while "soul surfing" took over as the sport's hip wave-riding ideal. Nobody knew exactly what "soul surfing" was, except that it represented another backlash to the sport's boom-era commercial growth. It was like localism in that respect. But where the hardcore local had a message ("my beach, my waves") and a plan (abuse nonlocals), the soul surfer existed in an anticommercial world of his own device. Most had no interest in competition, but some did. Most rode in a quieter and less-acrobatic style, but others jammed it out with the best of them. Most embraced similar countercultural social and political ideals, but nobody actively identified themselves as "soul surfers." The term had a squishy softness that eventually invited mockery. Yet for a time, it was everyone's easy shorthand for the widespread back-to-nature grassroots surf movement.

NAT YOUNG DURING HIS "COUNTRY SOUL" PHASE.

THE OVERSATURATED COLORS IN *MORNING OF THE EARTH*—SOUL SURFING'S DEFINING DOCUMENT—LOOK AS IF THEY WERE FILMED THROUGH A PSILOCYBIN GEL. WHICH WAS PRETTY MUCH THE CASE. AT BYRON BAY, WHERE ONE OF THE BEST *EARTH* SEQUENCES WAS FILMED, HALLUCINOGENIC MUSHROOMS WOULD SPRING UP FROM COW PATTIES AFTER A GOOD RAIN. "THE RULE IN OUR GROUP WAS SIMPLE," *EARTH* HEADLINER NAT YOUNG RECALLED. "IF ANYONE STUMBLED UPON A MUSHROOM WHILE WALKING DOWN TO CHECK THE SURF, THEY HAD TO EAT IT."

MORNING OF THE EARTH *BY ALBERT FALZON, 1972.*

A film by Albert Falzon

"We are the measure of all things.
And the beauty of our creation, of our art
is proportional to the beauty of ourselves
of our souls" Jonas Mekas

TERRY FITZGERALD AND MICHAEL PETERSON

"Performance surfing" is a loosely defined term, but it generally means a fast, active, dynamic style of riding in waves smaller than eight or ten feet. By the early seventies the Aussies were taking ownership of the category. Under-eighteen junior division champions like Mark Richards, Wayne Bartholomew, and Peter Townend—years before their respective primes—were outsurfing all but the best from California and Hawaii. The Aussie seniors (eighteen and above) were even better. There at the very top were Sydney's Terry Fitzgerald and Queensland's Michael Peterson. Fitzgerald did for performance surfing what Led Zeppelin did for the blues—he made the genre bigger, louder, heavier. He not only looked like Robert Plant, in fact, with his jutting chin and Viking mane of hair, he rode with the same lascivious hip-thrusting that Plant used on stage—the surf press called it "body torque," but it looked more like a grinding seduction. Peterson, meanwhile, was dark-eyed and brooding. He had the same lanky, wide-shouldered physique as Nat Young, and his hands and arms jumped around like severed powerlines when he surfed. Occasionally it was distracting. Mostly it accentuated Peterson's incredible balance. Like Phil Edwards, he would often push his turns to just past the breaking point and trust his reflexes to figure out a quick recovery. Fitzgerald and

Peterson both epitomized the Australian way of surfing: aggressive, flamboyant, even exaggerated, but with full mastery of the fundamentals.

TERRY FITZGERALD WITH NORTH SHORE QUIVER, 1975.

LARRY BERTLEMANN

Hawaii had its own supercharged high-performance savant in Waikiki's Larry Bertlemann. He was called the Rubberman, which was fitting; Bertlemann rode lower to the deck of his board than anybody before him, sometimes dropping his haunches nearly to his heels, and he was the first to understand that in order to lay out a really good, tight, full-circuit turn, you had to loosen up the torso and shoulders. From his afro-topped head to his amphibious toes, Bertlemann surfed as if he were spring-loaded. He pumped the effect up with brightly-colored boards, disco-leisure beachwear, and a confident line of patter. The flash and jive, in fact, could be blinding—Bertlemann once paddled into a crowded North Shore lineup wearing a custom-made bell-bottom wetsuit. But his contribution to the sport was enormous. Bertlemann reinvented the turn, and his approach—the low center of gravity, a swiveling upper body—was the starting point for all high-performance surfing to follow.

LARRY BERTLEMANN, ALA MOANA, 1975.

LOOKING THROUGH THE TUBE AT PIPELINE.

THROUGH EVERY CHANGE IN BOARD DESIGN AND RIDING STYLE, AND EVERY SHIFT IN SURFING'S GLOBAL BALANCE OF POWER, HAWAII NEVER LOST ITS LUSTER. THE NORTH SHORE OF OAHU REMAINED THE SPORT'S GREAT FINAL CHALLENGE, THE ULTIMATE DESTINATION. THE SHORTBOARD REVOLUTION DID NOTHING BUT UNDERSCORE THIS FACT, AND FROM 1969 TO 1976, VERY LITTLE HAPPENED IN THE SPORT THAT WASN'T SOME-HOW ALIGNED WITH RESPECT TO HAWAII.

PIPELINE

The shortboard revolution put tube-riding front and center as the ultimate surfing experience, and that would never change. Surfers occasionally found the tube during the fifties and sixties, but not until short surfboards were introduced did tube-riding become a kind of space race among the world's best surfers. Pipeline, the hollowest, ficklest, most dangerous break on Hawaii's North Shore, was at the center of the action. The wave at Pipeline was long thought impossible to surf. As one North Shore surfer said to another in the late fifties, "Two thousand years from now, maybe they'll be riding it." Phil Edwards of California, as it turned out, broke the ice in 1961, and from then on Pipeline, for many, became an obsession. A bare-knuckled surfer named Butch Van Artsdalen, also from California, put himself in the tube at Pipeline with some regularity during the midsixties, on a longboard, while switchfooting local boy Jock Sutherland set the pace during the first two years of the shortboard era. On the other hand, Joaquin Miro Quesada, one of Peru's best surfers, was thrown headfirst into the reef at Pipeline in 1967, broke his neck, and died a few hours later. As surfers have learned, Pipeline can be ridden, but it always exacts a toll.

PIPELINE WIPEOUT, 1966.

STARTING IN THE LATE 1960s, TUBE-RIDING GENERATED A CULT-LIKE FASCINATION AMONG SURFERS. IT WAS CALLED THE "GREEN CATHEDRAL." A *TALES FROM THE TUBE* COMIC BOOK WAS RELEASED. THE VIEW FROM INSIDE THE TUBE, ONE MOVIE REVIEWER WROTE, WAS NOTHING LESS THAN THE "CRYSTAL BATTLEMENTS WHEREIN THE DAEMON OF THE EARTH ENTRUSTED HIS TEMPLE."

TALES FROM THE TUBE, *A 1971* SURFER *COMIC BOOK INSERT.*

NORTH SHORE SURFERS

On the North Shore of Oahu, surfing's own mecca, a small group of Hawaiian surfers during the late sixties and the first half of the seventies were so much better than everybody else, and so relentlessly filmed and photographed, that the rest of the world's best often seemed massed together in the background. Teenager Michael Ho, not much over five feet tall, zapped up and down at Velzyland as if he were riding on a thin cushion of air. Pureblood Hawaiian Eddie Aikau rode gigantic Waimea Bay better than anyone before him. Reno Abellira crouched over his board like Bruce Lee facing down a gang of Hong Kong toughs and carved turns with Euclidean precision. At Sunset Beach, Barry Kanaiaupuni and Jeff Hakman were the yin and yang of power surfing. Kanaiaupuni used a narrow, almost delicate stance, feet and legs positioned in a kind of demi-plié, but he threw his board around like Ornette Coleman on a long free-jazz riff. Hakman, meanwhile, was all balance, utility, and faultless construction. He rode low and centered, arms extended from his muscle-packed shoulders like glider wings. You always knew what Hakman was going to do, and it was always perfect.

Then there was Pipeline ace Gerry Lopez, who reinvented tube-riding in his own silky-smooth image. In his best moments, Lopez didn't seem to be performing at all—or at least not in the way Hakman, Kanaiaupuni, and the rest performed. He stood quietly, hands and arms relaxed at his sides, knees just slightly bent, face calm. He wasn't the first less-is-more surfer. But he did it in the ionized center of Pipeline tubes that exploded around him like cannon fire—making the most difficult thing in the sport appear like a meditation.

PIPELINE.

GERRY LOPEZ, PIPELINE, 1972.

A TINY SLIVER OF DAYLIGHT EXISTED AT THE TOP OF THE HAWAIIAN SURFER PANTHEON, AND THERE, SLENDER AS GANDHI, STOOD GERRY LOPEZ—THE COOLEST SURFER ALIVE; THE PIPELINE FIREWALKER; THE MAN WHO SINGLE-HANDEDLY RAISED THE TUBE-RIDE FROM A MERE SURFING MANEUVER TO AN ADVANCED ZEN PRACTICE.

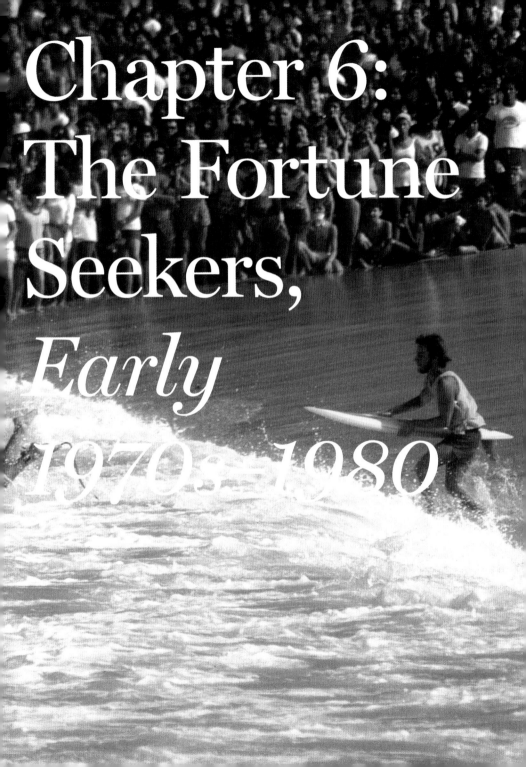

Chapter 6:
The Fortune
Seekers,
Early
1970s–1980

EXOTIC SURF TRAVEL

Exotic surf travel was a 1960s invention. Up to then, the only full-dress surf excursion was the odd steamer trip across the Pacific to Hawaii. Even that was a voyage to the great known, not the great unknown. In 1963, Australian Peter Troy set out on his first and longest transnational adventure, which he afterward described in a *Surfer* article entitled, "Around the World on a Surfboard." The 125,000-mile journey was filled with great waves and new friendships—and a few jaunty indiscretions, such as when Troy was jailed briefly in Brazil on a gold-smuggling charge and offered work as a Monte Carlo gigolo. That was also the year Bruce Brown jetted off to film *The Endless Summer*. Brown's movie burned so brightly as the model of first-generation surf travel that other adventures—including a dozen or so well-reported trips that had preceded it—were by and large struck from the record.

Then the shortboard revolution arrived, and exotic surf became the sport's holy grail. Part of it was the equipment. A 7-foot, 10-pound spacestick was so much easier to travel with than a signature model noserider. Mostly, though, it was the tenor of the times. Just about every buzz-phrase of the period—"do your own thing," "soul surfing," "back to nature"— was an invitation to pack up and go, to feed your head with new places and experiences, and to score some hot, uncrowded waves. Drugs played a part. In the late sixties and throughout the seventies, probably half of the hardcore surf travelers were moonlighting as dope smugglers, or vice-versa. Many of those who weren't trafficking were at least encouraged by the thought of visiting places where the highs were cheap and often legal.

BERNIE BAKER, EL SALVADOR, 1970.

INDONESIA

In the midseventies, surfers everywhere were becoming familiar with Uluwatu, a glistening temple-fronted break located on the southwest corner of Bali. The Aussies, as was so often the case during this period, were on it first. Denpasar, Bali's capital city, was a relatively easy five-hour flight from Sydney—closer than Hawaii was to California. Even for the experienced traveler, Bali was overwhelmingly exotic. Small baskets of flowers and incense were laid out daily by the thousands, on front steps, sidewalks, street corners, and countertops. Terraced rice fields covered the hills like multi-acre pieces of Art Deco emerald jewelry, and the air was perfumed with frangipani and tuberose, wood smoke and incense. Ten thousand stonework temples covered the island, many of them huge and ornate and covered in fanged, grinning, pop-eyed demons. What about the surf at Uluwatu? Heart-stopping. A blue-on-blue, cliff-lined panorama of long, fast, hollow, left-breaking waves. A sun-kissed dreamscape. Not as powerful as the North Shore, but smoother and better groomed. Best of all, Uluwatu was clearly just the opening act. Indonesia is a 2,500-mile-long chain of perfect waves awaiting discovery. Nearly five decades later, surfers are still finding never-before-surfed breaks here.

PETER MCCABE, ULUWATU, BALI.

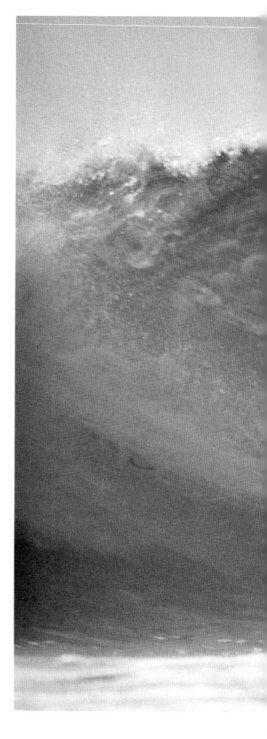

SUPERTUBES, JEFFREYS BAY.

JEFFREYS BAY, IN SOUTH AFRICA, IS ISOLATED, COLD, SHARK-INFESTED, AND WIND-TORN. IN THE EARLY SEVENTIES, IT WAS ALSO HOME TO A BREAK THAT MADE EVERYBODY'S SHORT LIST FOR "WORLD'S BEST WAVE."

THE BIRTH OF PROFESSIONAL SURFING

Professional surfing originated in the midseventies, but it had a brief trial run of sorts a decade earlier. In 1965, Midget Farrelly earned $8,000 from endorsement deals. David Nuuhiwa, Nat Young, and Gary Propper all got royalty checks for their signature model surfboards. Eighteen-year-old Corky Carroll, even before he'd won the first of three US Surfing Championships titles, put "professional surfer" on his 1965 tax return. Awards for a 1965 contest in Redondo Beach included a motorcycle, a color TV, a wardrobe, and Timex watches, and that year's July Fourth weekend brought the first cash-prize event: the $1,500 Tom Morey Invitational in Ventura.

The Duke Kahanamoku Invitational gave pro surfing its first real beachhead. When the contest debuted at Sunset Beach in 1965, it was a revelation: an event designed for big North Shore surf. No money was on offer, but the elite one-day contest was a huge hit—and seventeen-year-old high schooler Jeff Hakman was a popular winner. Two years later, during the early stages of the shortboard revolution, as California was being portrayed as the evil empire of surfing commercialism, it became obvious that pro surfing needed a change of venue. The Duke was a perfect fit. It allowed the whole movement to quietly shift its base of operation to Hawaii, and it bumped up the drama considerably. The West Coast pro contests were nearly all held in small, garden-variety surf, which made for dull spectating. The competitors themselves strongly believed that money events should be held in the best waves possible—and in the late 1960s, that meant Hawaii. Media outlets agreed. ABC's *Wide World of Sports* had covered the California pro contests, but in 1968 the network dropped West Coast surfing altogether and rushed off to the North Shore to tape the Duke contest which, for the first time, offered a winner-take-all cash prize of $1,000 to the winner.

TOP: JEFF HAKMAN IN YELLOW TRUNKS, 1972 DUKE KAHANAMOKU INVITATIONAL.

BOTTOM: CORKY CARROLL (RIGHT), 1965 LAGUNA MASTERS.

PRO SURFING IN THE MIDSEVENTIES WAS A LONG WAY FROM THE BIG TIME. "I REMEMBER BORROWING MONEY FROM PRETTY MUCH EVERYBODY I KNEW," TWO-TIME PIPELINE MASTERS WINNER RORY RUSSELL SAID. "LIKE, 'HEY, MOM, COULD I HAVE $600 TO GO TO AUSTRALIA?'"

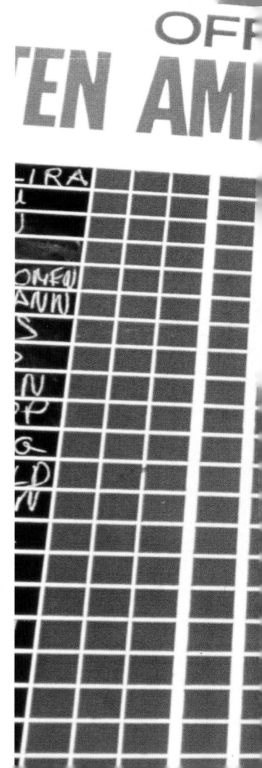

1974 AMERICAN PRO CHAMPIONSHIPS, SUNSET BEACH.

IAL SCOREBOARD
ICAN PRO CHAMP
ROUND I
HEAT I
D. GOMEZ
P. NIELSON
I. CAIRNS
R. RUSSELL
J. HAKMAN
E AIKAU
M PURPUS
B. AIPA

HEMMING TAKES CHARGE

Former world champion Fred Hemmings of Hawaii was a county chairman for the Republican Party in 1976 when he took the lead in stringing together a group of disparate pro contests from around the world into a "pro surfing tour" that would decide a world champion. In 1972, the single-event World Surfing Championships had imploded, and Hemmings believed that surfing needed to reintroduce the idea, but with prize money and ratings points. So in the summer of 1976, with help from fellow Hawaiian and part-time pro surfer Randy Rarick, Hemmings held regular meetings, usually in the kitchen of Rarick's rented North Shore flat, and created an organization they called International Professional Surfers—or the IPS tour for short. Hemmings became the executive director. He handled event sponsors, media, and anything else having to do with nonsurfing parties. Rarick was the administrative director; he dealt mostly with the surfers, which initially meant wheedling a $5 IPS registration fee from each pro.

The tricky part was choosing which events to include, and how to rank surfers, when the year was already half over. Hemmings wanted to rank the pros by their prize-money earnings. Aussie pro surfers Ian Cairns and Peter Townend, however, convinced Hemmings to adopt the same points-based ratings system that was used in professional tennis and Formula One racing. For 1976, Rarick went over the result sheets for all the pro contests held worldwide since January, and he retroactively placed nine events into that year's contest schedule: three in Australia, two in South Africa, and one each in Brazil, New Zealand, Florida, and Hawaii. He also calculated each surfer's point total so far. In other words, the tour was two-thirds finished before anybody knew it existed, and the season would end with the five upcoming North Shore events in Hawaii. Gathered together, the tour events resembled a jumble sale: contest formats and judging systems changed from event to event, as did the number of surfers allowed to compete. At season's end, furthermore, Townend and Cairns finished as world champion and runner-up, respectively. Sure, they were both top surfers, but they'd also helped create the tour they'd just won. Despite a bit of head-shaking over that, however, the pros liked the idea of having a circuit of events and a world title to shoot for. The pro tour would keep working out the kinks for years to come, but pro surfing became a growth industry from that point on.

FRED HEMMINGS (RIGHT), INTERVIEWED BY BRUCE JENNER, MID-1970s.

MARGO OBERG, SUNSET BEACH.

TWENTY-FIVE PRO TOUR WOMEN'S EVENTS WERE HELD BETWEEN 1977 AND 1981. MARGO OBERG AND LYNNE BOYER, BETWEEN THEM, WON TWENTY. NO OTHER FEMALE PRO WAS EVEN IN THE GAME.

WAYNE BARTHOLOMEW AND MARK RICHARDS

Two Australians—along with South African Shaun Tomson—dominated the pro tour's early years. In Australia, Queensland's Wayne Bartholomew, the 1978 world champion, was the scrappiest and the most entertaining of the new pros, drawing inspiration—and occasional wardrobe choices—from David Bowie, Muhammad Ali, Mick Jagger, and Bilbo Baggins. At a time when a lot of other pros were trying to clean up their act so as to make surfing more presentable to a hoped-for mainstream audience, Bartholomew kept his hair in a surfer-shag and drove a $50 Holden sedan with see-through floorboards. He was the people's champ. Mark Richards of Newcastle, New South Wales, rode in a strange knock-kneed stance, but he was the era's best-tuned high-performance surfer. He had his great trial-by-fire moment in late 1974, when he flew to Hawaii as a rookie and unexpectedly got a start in that year's Smirnoff Pro-Am. The first day of competition was held in medium-sized waves at Sunset Beach, and Richards aced his prelim heat. After a lay period, the contest venue was switched to Waimea Bay, as a thirty-foot-plus swell filed in. Richards swallowed hard, paddled out, didn't win, but held his own. He was just seventeen years old. Four years later, Richards popularized the long-dormant twin-fin board design, which pushed along his stated desire to "rip, tear, and lacerate," and he did just that during an astonishing world title run that lasted from 1979 to 1982. While Richards surfed with thundering power and torque, in waves of all sizes, he was the sweetest and most affable of the new pros. He graciously retired after winning his fourth title, at age twenty-five, saying, "I have no desire to bust down anymore doors." He said he thought of himself as "an ordinary person who can stand on a surfboard very well."

MARK RICHARDS AND WAYNE BARTHOLOMEW, BELLS BEACH, 1979.

P CURL
RK RICH
NE BA
OSON
QUARTER
DANE
EALOHA
BRUCE
AYMOND
HEAT 4
BRIAN

SHAUN TOMSON

Shaun Tomson of Durban, South Africa, won the 1977 world title, but he really made his mark as a tube-riding savant. Gerry Lopez, for years, was the ultimate tube-rider. His board flew straight as a spear through the hollows, while Lopez stood in motionless repose. Nothing in the sport was as beautiful, and Tomson himself was happy to do the point-and-shoot. But it was an approach that worked best in big, wide-open, well-shaped tubes. To ride deep inside a less-than-perfect tube—or to ride deeper inside a perfect one, for that matter—meant the surfer had to be more active, had to turn and bob and weave. Tomson did just that by widening his stance, effectively allowing him to both trim or turn at will, and thus he invented the "pump" style of riding the tube. He also worked on a board with extra lift in the nose and tail, which cost him in terms of flat-out speed but brought huge gains in control while in the tube. With all these advantages, Tomson worked out a number of ways to extend his time inside the barrel—all of which were shown off to mesmerizing effect in Bill Delaney's *Free Ride*, the essential film document of surfing in the midseventies. When the pro circuit was launched in 1976, Tomson finished in sixth place—he'd missed a lot of the events, partly because he was going to school, and partly because, like most pros, he had no idea there was going to be a world title that year until just a few weeks before it was handed out. Competing full-time in 1977, Tomson took the crown. It wasn't a walk in the park, exactly; Wayne Bartholomew led the ratings up until Hawaii. But Tomson was already the world's best surfer—the championship only rubber-stamped this fact.

SHAUN TOMSON, BACKDOOR PIPELINE, 1975.

LA JOLLA SURFERS ON A 1972 MIDWINTER ROAD TRIP, DURING CALIFORNIA'S "UNDERGROUND" PERIOD.

IN THE 1970s, SURFERS WERE STILL TRYING TO CALIBRATE THEIR DEFINITION OF EXACTLY WHAT THEY WERE DOING; FOR A DECADE AFTER THE SHORTBOARD WAS INTRODUCED, THEY ENGAGED IN A NONSTOP ANGELS-DANCING-ON-THE-HEAD-OF-A-PIN DEBATE AS TO WHETHER SURFING WAS A "SPORT" OR AN "ART."

Chapter 7:
The Long
and the Short

RETURN OF LONGBOARDING

In 1970, with shortboard revolutionaries still waving the torches used to incinerate the previous era—which included not just longboards, but boom-age surf culture in its entirety—the idea of longboarding was laughable. "Have you walked up to one of those antiques lately and tried to pick it up?" *Surfing World* magazine asked its readers in 1970. "Or for that matter, pictured yourself trying to actually ride one?" Yet the shortboard revolution was flawed: tens of thousands of surfers became frustrated with the twitchy new boards, and the new hippie-heavy surf-world vibe, and they gave up the sport altogether. Meanwhile, at surf breaks around the world, an endless stream of longboard-friendly waves—one-to-two-foot peelers that didn't quite have the energy to power up the latest equipment—rolled through untouched. The shortboard revolution was nearly as wasteful as it was exciting.

In hindsight, nothing in the sport's history seems as logical or inevitable as the comeback of longboarding, which started in the midseventies and really gained momentum throughout the eighties. Even

Bob McTavish and Nat Young, two of the original shortboarders, returned to longboarding in small waves. "It's much more fun than it looks," McTavish noted in 1977, "and it looks like fun." Everybody said the same thing: longboarding was a return to "fun" surfing. Catching lots of waves, cross-stepping, spinners, no-effort trim—it was a blast. Also, longboarding was the only way to go if you were overweight or out of shape, and that included thousands of surfers who'd quit the sport in the late sixties. Finally, longboarding was also an antidote to localism, pro tour careerism, windy soul-surfing pieties, and all the rest of the accumulated seriousness that had grown like vines over the sport during the previous twenty years. In California, regional pride was involved, too. Sure, longboarding was a retro trend. But California had more longboard surfers, clubs, and contests than anywhere in the world. When at last the state made a surfing comeback, the longboard was a big part of it.

LONGBOARD REVIVALIST BEN AIPA, WAIKIKI, 1979.

SIMON ANDERSON AND THE THRUSTER

In early 1981, Simon Anderson, a lantern-jawed pro surfer from Narrabeen, New South Wales, introduced a new type of board he winkingly called the "Thruster." He claimed the name wasn't a sexual double entendre. Nobody believed him. Anderson's board was a peculiar-looking craft, with a narrow nose and three small fins placed in a triangular cluster near the tail. People seeing it for the first time actually laughed out loud, and not without reason. Over the previous fifteen years or so, there had been no end to the flow of surfboard design "innovations," the vast majority of which were at best half-baked and sank without a trace. At first glance, the Thruster didn't seem any different. But Anderson, a top shaper as well as a water-gouging power surfer, quickly proved that his new design was something very special indeed. At Bells Beach that Easter, in huge surf, during the Rip Curl Pro world tour contest, Anderson paddled out and changed the course of surf history. The twin-fin riders on their jittery little boards looked as if they'd been pushed down a steep driveway in shopping carts. The best of the single-finners drew the kind of long, elegant lines that would have been new and exciting in 1971. On his airbrushed-blue, 6-foot 6-inch Thruster, Anderson accelerated and cornered like a Formula One race car, all speed, power, and control, with his board stuck to the huge Bells faces as if it were magnetized. He won going away. Within a year, nearly every touring pro had jumped over to an Anderson-style board. The Thruster—better known, in years to come, as the tri-fin—became the biggest surfboard breakthrough since the shortboard revolution.

SIMON ANDERSON, NARRABEEN.

ON CHRISTMAS EVE, 1981, A TWENTY-FIVE-YEAR-OLD WET-SUIT-CLAD MONTEREY COUNTY KNEEBOARDER NAMED LEW BOREN WAS PULLED FROM THE SHALLOWS OF PACIFIC GROVE. HIS BODY WAS BLOODLESS, WITH A PERFECTLY SYMMET-RICAL ARMPIT-TO-HIP BITE TAKEN OUT OF HIS TORSO—THE WORK OF A TWENTY-FOOT-LONG, FOUR-THOUSAND-POUND WHITE SHARK. BOREN WAS CALIFOR-NIA SURFING'S FIRST SHARK FATALITY.

LEW BOREN'S SHARK-BITTEN KNEEBOARD, MONTEREY, CALIFORNIA, 1981.

A BILLION-DOLLAR SPORT

The 1980s brought the sport its biggest popularity boom since *Endless Summer*. There were surf bars in Manhattan, surf-themed frat house parties, even a new version of *Gidget* on TV. Mostly there was surfwear. Quiksilver, Ocean Pacific, Gotcha, and the rest of the hot surf labels powered the sport's hard-charging new economy and together formed what news sources in 1986 called a "billion-dollar industry." Most of the money came from inland states. A college professor said that surfing was a "mass-culture fantasy" and that "mental surfing" should be encouraged as "a relief from everyday stress." That was one way of looking at it. Asked by a *Los Angeles Times* reporter what the new heartland surf craze was all about, a thirteen-year-old from St. Louis shrugged and said, "Everybody wants to go to the beach, but it's five hundred miles away."

QUIKSILVER AD SHOOT, NEWPORT BEACH, CALIFORNIA, EARLY EIGHTIES.

TOM CARROLL AND
TOM CURREN

Australia's Tom Carroll met California teenager Tom Curren in the finals of the 1982 Marui Pro in Chiba, Japan. Pros, judges, clued-in fans, the surf media—everybody that day understood the significance of this matchup. Curren and Carroll represented the future of high-end surfing. The world tour had plenty of talented surfers, but everything you needed to know about the sport's performance trajectory for the rest of the decade could be graphed on Tom Carroll's muscle-flexing turn combinations and Tom Curren's ethereal flow and technique. "And so a new era gets underway," surf journalist Paul Holmes wrote. "If I were a betting man, I'd be putting my money on one of these guys to take next year's world championship—and, between the two of them, another few titles after that." It was a safe bet. Carroll won the title in 1983 and 1984; Curren won the two after that and added a third crown in 1990.

Carroll, the fitness-obsessed goofy-footer, was just five foot six, 145 pounds, but nonetheless recognized as a purebred power surfer. As quick and sharp as he was in smaller waves, he didn't come into full devastating form until the surf was overhead, and on Oahu's North Shore—the better part of Carroll's reputation was made at Sunset Beach and Pipeline—he put his turns together with the slashing, brutal elegance of Jim Brown on an open-field run. Carroll's turns "were so powerful," one surf journalist wrote, "they left vapor trails." Curren was powerful as well, but the force was often concealed behind a riding style that, even in his teens, was surpassingly graceful and flowing. He combined the two dominate stylistic themes from the previous decade—the cool, purified elegance of Gerry Lopez and the "rip, tear, and lacerate" attack of the Australians. Furthermore, Tom, like his famous big-wave-riding father, Pat, was quietly enigmatic—an antidote to the Aussie bluster and swagger that had been in vogue the past few years. Finally, Curren was a West Coaster, which was a huge plus for those yearning for the end of the "California Surfing Ice Age," as one surf mag put it.

TOM CARROLL, WINKIPOP, VICTORIA, 1989.

**RADICAL SURFING WAS
NO BIG DEAL IN THE
1980s. RADICAL AND
ETHEREAL—THAT WAS
TOM CURREN, AND
ONLY CURREN. "HE'S
ON ANOTHER LEVEL,"
ONE MAGAZINE PUT IT.
"HE CAN SURF A WAVE
THE WAY THE REST OF
US ONLY MIND-SURF IT."**

TOM CURREN, HOSSEGOR, FRANCE, 1991.

AUSTRALIA'S ENDLESS TALENT

Through the late '70s and early '80s, Australia, more than any other surfing region, continued to shape and define the sport. Nine men's division world titles were handed out between 1976 and 1984—eight went to Aussies. Australia was home to the coolest (and soon to be biggest) names in the surf industry, including Rip Curl, Quiksilver, and Billabong. Under the editorship of Nick Carroll (Tom's older brother), Sydney-based *Tracks* magazine was regarded by insiders as surfing's best publication. Aussie slang even pushed out a lot of American-coined favorites—"grommet" replaced "gremmie," and "boardshorts" was clearly a better, more surfy term than "trunks." Surfing had become seamlessly merged into Australia's national identity. Unlike in the United States, Australian newspapers and magazines generally looked at surfers not as offbeat curiosities or beachfront thugs but as fully integrated sportsmen—to a point, actually, where surfing too often seemed defined by heat scores and year-end standings. Aussie flamboyance, meanwhile, was the rule for a generation of pros who came of age in the 1980s. Gary Elkerton told an interviewer that his American counterparts were "a bunch of softcocks." Seventeen-year-old Mark Occhilupo, in his first *Surfer* portrait, grinned like a jack-o-lantern while caressing a bottle of champagne tucked into his jacket. Sydney surf journalist John Witzig fondly remembered young Tom Carroll reacting to his first Surfabout heat-draw by "jumping three feet into the air, roaring with lust, and twisting his face into an aggro expression of ambition." One-upping their *Free Ride* predecessors, the new Aussie pros made the surf world a louder, showier, more colorful place.

TOP: GARY "KONG" ELKERTON, 1984.

BOTTOM: MARK OCCHILUPO.

FLYBOY MARTIN POTTER

Young world-tour pro Martin Potter was the first of his generation to realize that the era's new moves could be served up with a new attitude. In 1983, at age seventeen, he had the brass to call out fellow world-tour newcomer Tom Curren for having "a conservative approach," and he said the same about four-time world champion Mark Richards, for good measure. Potter's own method was based on "going for big moves and taking risks. I just can't approach a wave conservatively. It's just not in me. If I don't go out and pull off at least one aerial, I'm not happy." In 1985, Potter spent the summer at San Clemente, an Orange County beach town. He was in full-throttle aerial mode, ready to vault off any likely-looking curl that came his way. Wipeouts didn't matter. Hang time did. Matt Archbold and Christian Fletcher, two local schoolboy groms, watched carefully. In the coming years, as Potter turned the volume down in order to pick up a world championship, Archbold and Fletcher took the aerial and expanded it into a loud, slightly delinquent surfing subspecies—just as noseriding had been two decades earlier.

HIGH-FLYING MARTIN POTTER.

Surfing turned ever-more garish and gaudy during the 1980s, and one manifestation of this was the Op Pro, a Labor Day weekend world tour surf contest first held in 1982. Ocean Pacific beachwear underwrote the event to the tune of $400,000—ten times more than any other contest on the schedule that year. Op wanted noise and bombast, sideshows and huge crowds. They wanted a VIP area with laminated access passes, front-page sports section coverage, and the Goodyear blimp. In short, they wanted the Superbowl of pro surfing contests.

That's exactly what they got. In 1982, the weather was perfect, and thirty-five thousand people cheered Cheyne Horan to victory over Shaun Tomson in the finals—with the Goodyear blimp, sure enough, floating overhead. Contest director and just-retired pro Ian Cairns said the Op Pro would bring a "massive payoff" for surfing's world tour, and he was right. New sponsors rushed forward, and within two years the number of men's division events doubled, from twelve to twenty-four. Not everybody was thrilled.

By putting spectacle first, the pros were often forced out into sub-par waves. Surfing almost became secondary to the expo booths, the product displays, the half-pipe ramp, the Jet Ski show, and the bikini contest. Yet the events kept growing—right up until the 1986 Op Pro, when a female spectator had her top yanked down behind the bleachers. Police were called, rocks were thrown, and an hour later, less than a hundred yards from the contest site, thousands of rioters set cars on fire, smashed windows at the lifeguard headquarters, and held off more than 150 baton-wielding police reinforcements. "The great mainstream experiment has failed," a *Surfer* editorial declared. Forget the big crowds, the magazine advised; wave-riding isn't like other sports. As presented on the world circuit, surfing had come to resemble nothing so much as a "plug horse in a straw hat, straining for the unobtainable carrot dangling in front of its nose."

TOM CURREN, IN ORANGE VEST, 1984 OP PRO.

TAVARUA

The first surf camp opened in the late 1970s, on the edge of a Javanese jungle, at a world-class break called Grajagan. The living was fairly primitive—bamboo huts and netting, lots of rice, a generator or two—but the idea that surfers would pay to have access to great waves, the way golfers paid to stay at Pebble Beach, was a small revelation. It made perfect sense. Surfers, on average, were getting older and wealthier. Lineups at home were getting more crowded. Why not pay to play? By the mideighties, the surf resort idea gained momentum. While most remained down-market, the Tavarua Island Resort in Fiji was described—usually with longing, sometimes with disdain—as surfing's version of Club Med. The nearby breaks, of course, were stunning, and the tiny heart-shaped island itself was the very definition of tropical paradise. Beyond that, Tavarua Resort guests had private rooms, clean bedding, a full staff, and a restaurant-bar. "Tavarua," Australian surf journalist Tim Baker wrote after his first stay on the island, was "the world's most satisfying surfing experience." Customers agreed. From 1985 on, Tavarua Resort reservations had to be made months, even years, in advance.

RESTAURANT'S LINEUP, TAVARUA, WITH TAVARUA ISLAND RESORT IN THE FOREGROUND.

APARTHEID

When it comes to politics, the surfer's default position has always been, "Sports and politics don't mix." Politics is by and large viewed as something you escape by going surfing. But in the mideighties, a number of top surfers roused themselves, temporarily anyway, from their political apathy to protest against apartheid in South Africa. It started in 1985, when reigning world champion Tom Carroll told an Australian newspaper that he was going to boycott that year's three-event South African leg of the pro tour. Carroll was a classic "fair go" Aussie; he'd been to South Africa four times already and didn't like what he'd seen. "The father of a guy I surfed with there once told me we were lucky in Australia," Carroll wrote in his autobiography, "[because] all our Aborigines had been killed." Carroll also knew that Hawaiian pro Dane Kealoha had been ordered from a whites-only restaurant in Durban, and another Hawaiian surfer was beaten up at a disco for talking to a white woman. Boycotting the South African contests, Carroll said, was simply "a basic humanitarian stand." Within a few days, Carroll's boycott was joined by Tom Curren, Cheyne Horan, and Martin Potter, pro surfing's fourth-, fifth-, and sixth-ranked surfers, respectively.

World tour officials didn't blink, and the pro circuit continued making annual stops in South Africa through apartheid's final years (apartheid ended in 1994)—even while the prize money was reduced, the number of boycotters went up, and magazines like *Surfer* dropped their coverage of the South African contests altogether. In 1985, despite missing the three South African contests, Curren went on to take that year's world title. Tom Carroll would later be praised for his political courage by no less a figure than Australian prime minister Bob Hawke. For a brief moment, the world's best surfers were engaged with the rest of the world—and played a bit part in South Africa's anti-apartheid struggles.

DURBAN, SOUTH AFRICA, 1966.

AN INTERNATIONAL SWELL

During the 1980s and early 1990s, surfing developed worldwide at a happy, ambling pace, reflecting a growing international embrace of the sport. Vetea David of Tahiti won the juniors' division of the 1986 World Surfing Championships. Tel Aviv was home to five thousand surfers, and a few dozen Italian *ragazzi* were thrashing around in the mostly choppy waves off of Livorno, Viareggio, and Genoa.

The Swedish Surfing Association was up and running. A Norse fireman named Roar Berge was tackling the reefs and points near Stavanger, Norway. German lifeguards were shooting the shorebreak in the North Sea. From a short distance, Peru's euphoniously-named Luis Miguel "Magoo" de la Rosa, a seven-time national champion from Lima, could be mistaken for Tom Carroll.

Surfing grew everywhere, though faster in some places than others. After Quiksilver Europe opened a retail outlet in Biarritz in 1985, the town became France's version of Orange County, filled with surf shops, surf-themed restaurant and bars, and huge retail outlets for Billabong, Rip Curl, and others. The Biarritz surf wasn't too hot. But Hossegor's board-snapping tubes were only a few miles to the north, and just across the Spanish border, not far from Bilbao, at the mouth of the Guernica Estuary, long, fast, time-warping barrels could be had at a place called Mundaka.

CHICAMA, PERU.

EDDIE AIKAU

Big-wave surfing fell out of favor during the late sixties shortboard revolution, as surfers worldwide rushed to test the limits of high-performance surfing. Despite this, the seventies brought a final flourish in the career of Eddie Aikau, one the sport's defining big-wave riders. Aikau was a friendly but shy Catholic-raised Hawaiian. He spoke in a deep pidgin-laced mumble and lived with his big working-class family in a secluded house next to a Chinese graveyard, a few miles behind downtown Honolulu.

On a huge day at Waimea in 1966, Aikau rode for six straight hours and caught over a dozen twenty-footers. He was a twenty-year-old line worker at the Dole Pineapple cannery—and it was his first time at Waimea. Ten months later he returned and casually dominated the biggest day of the year, riding in his trademarked bow-legged stance, his arms extended and quiet. From that point on, Aikau was big-wave surfing's one-man elite, though competition wasn't a big deal to him. A North Shore lifeguard, Aikau notched his first and only North Shore contest win in late 1977, taking the Duke Kahanamoku Classic at Sunset Beach at the age of thirty-one. He'd recently become involved in the Hawaiian Renaissance movement, which worked to revive traditional Hawaiian arts and culture, and he was training as a crew member for the *Hokule'a*, a replica of a 60-foot Polynesian voyaging canoe. The plan was to sail it, using ancient navigational techniques, from Hawaii to Tahiti. In mid-March 1978—three months after he won the Duke contest—Aikau was aboard the *Hokule'a* when it overturned in heavy seas twenty miles west of Lanai. The radio and all provisions were lost. Twelve hours after capsizing, Aikau got on his board—he'd planned on surfing once in Tahiti—and began to paddle for Lanai, intending to get help for the crew. He was never seen again. By 1978, big-wave riding was a full decade into its long interregnum. With Eddie Aikau gone, the whole thing couldn't help but further collapse in on itself.

EDDIE AIKAU, WAIMEA.

ALEC COOKE JUMPED OUT OF A HELICOPTER FOR THIS
1984 SESSION AT THIRD REEF PIPELINE

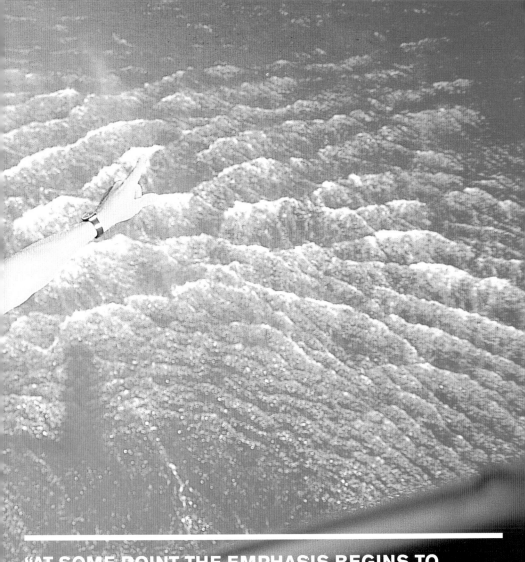

"AT SOME POINT THE EMPHASIS BEGINS TO CHANGE," GREG NOLL SAID, PREDICTING IN 1970 THAT THE SPORT'S OBSESSIVE FOCUS ON HIGH PERFORMANCE SURFING WOULD HAVE TO GIVE WAY. "AND WHAT'S LEFT IS A BIG, DAMN, TERRORIZING WAVE."

RETURN OF BIG-WAVE SURFING

Big-wave surfing's comeback started in 1983, following a long El Niño-fueled run of big waves generated in the North Pacific. In the aftermath, *Surfer* put together a four-article package under a banner headline reading "MONSTER SURF!" The magazine flipped over on its back like a puppy and rolled around in the drama. The hype was there in the images: huge Waimea, glassy Point Surf Makaha, a rugged big-wave rider holding the two pieces of his snapped board, another kneeling in prayer on the beach at Waimea before paddling out. The text pushed the theme just as hard. Big-wave riders, the magazine said, lived on "an ultra-level us regular surfers aren't even aware of." They were the surfing equivalent of fighter pilots, "strapped into their winged chemical bombs, primed to light the fuse and charge." In the beginning, much of big-wave surfing's Second Age was taken straight out of deep freeze from twenty years earlier. Waimea was still the ultimate break, and some of the big-wave originals from the fifties and sixties were still in the lineup. But there were new elements, too. New faces, like Mark Foo and Alec Cooke (alongside big-wave holdovers from the seventies like James Jones and Ken Bradshaw), and even new breaks, like Mexico's Todos Santos. Big-wave professionalism had its organized coming-out party in early 1986, with the Quiksilver/ Eddie Aikau Big-Wave Invitational— the first event designed specifically for Waimea Bay. Foo, Darrick Doerner, and a ropey eighteen-year-old named Brock Little were all standouts. But the $5,000 Quiksilver first-place check went to a teary Clyde Aikau, who rode a ten-year-old board that once belonged to his older brother, Eddie. Drama was the name of the game. Big-wave surfing, from that point forward, went from strength to strength.

ALEC COOKE'S AIRBORNE 11-FOOT BOARD.

Chapter 8: The Ride of Your Life, *1990–2015*

LISA ANDERSEN AND THE ROXY GIRL

Women surfers have had a rough go in surfing since . . . pretty much forever. The nineties brought some improvement, starting with the long-anticipated rise of Lisa Andersen, a smooth, powerful, stylish regularfooter, originally from Florida, who turned pro in 1987. After struggling for her first few years, Andersen won the first of four consecutive world championship titles in 1994 (one year after having a baby). She also became the face of Roxy, a division of surfwear giant Quiksilver, whose mission was to present female surfing as fashionable, sexy, and athletic—a "lifestyle," to use the advertising argot, upon which they hoped to build a billion-dollar juniors beachwear empire. A "Roxy Girl" team was put together, and the following ad campaign showed the girls (aged sixteen to twenty, mostly) riding longboards in plastic hula skirts and palm-frond hats, cruising the boardwalk on skateboards, and making pancake breakfast in their bikinis. The timing was perfect. After two decades, the feminist-first sportswoman model, as epitomized by Martina Navratilova, had run its course, and sex appeal—hetero all the way—was becoming an unabashed part of female athletics. Women would henceforth get a higher profile in surfing. But first in line—not necessarily for the world title, but for sponsorships, magazine shots, and in years to come social media "likes" and "follows"—were the girly-girls.

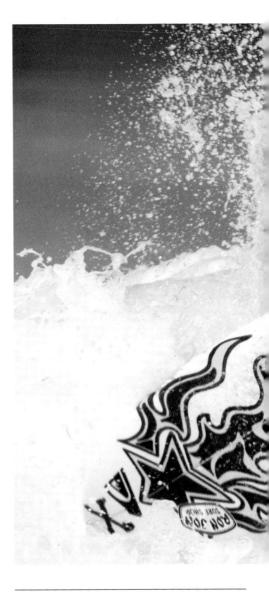

LISA ANDERSEN, 1995.

WOMEN'S SURFWEAR EXPLODED IN THE 1990S, AND SALES EVENTUALLY OUT-STRIPPED THE MEN'S LINES. LOOKING BACK A FEW YEARS LATER, SURF WRITER SAM GEORGE CHORTLED OVER THIS BUSI-NESS-MODEL TURN-AROUND. "SUDDENLY, AN INCREDIBLY GEN-DER-BIASED INDUS-TRY WOKE UP AND SAID, 'WAIT A MINUTE. WOMEN BUY *WAY* MORE CLOTHING AND ACCESSORIES THAN GUYS. WHAT WERE WE THINKING?'"

ROXY AD SHOOT, HUNTINGTON BEACH.

Kelly Slater came of age as a pro at the same time as fellow Floridian Lisa Andersen, and by the late 1990s, both were arguably the best male and female surfers ever—up to that time, at least. But where Andersen's career tapered off after that, Slater reached that mark and just kept ascending. He didn't just break competition records; he ran the numbers up until they seemed disconnected from those of his superstar peers. World titles, for instance: Tom Carroll had two, Tom Curren had three, Mark Richards had four. Slater won six in the 1990s, took a three-year break, then came back and picked up another five. In 1992, at age twenty, Slater was the youngest-ever male pro world champion, and in 2011, at age thirty-nine, he became the oldest. Slater didn't have anything even resembling a weak spot in his game. His turns were both powerful and fluid; his aerial moves were complex and futuristic. Origami-like body positioning allowed Slater to ride deeper in the tube, especially on his backhand, even in cataclysmic double-suck barrels at Pipeline. "He invents things so fast," *Surfing* magazine said, "people have trouble naming them."

Over the course of his long career, Kelly Slater has played guitar onstage with Pearl Jam; made the cover of *Sports Illustrated, Interview,* and *Outside;* starred in his own PlayStation video game; was rendered in twenty-foot-high statuary; and made *Hard Day's Night*-like escapes from crying mobs of female fans. Bruce Weber photographed him. Cocoa Beach named a street in his honor. On *Surfer*'s 2009 list of the fifty greatest surfers of all time, Slater finished on top. (Duke Kahanamoku placed second; Tom Curren third.) He dated, in order, Pamela Anderson, Gisele Bündchen, and Cameron Diaz. "He is, with absolutely no equivocation, the biggest surf star of the modern era," one surf journalist said. "How utterly convenient that he is also the best wave-rider."

KELLY SLATER, OFF-THE-WALL, 1992.

BEFORE ANDY IRONS, SLATER NEVER HAD A RIVAL WORTHY OF THE NAME. IRONS, WITH HIS THREE WORLD TITLES, DEMANDED ALL OF SLATER'S ATTENTION. IRONS WAS BORN IN A COOL GUNSLINGER CROUCH, WITH A MASSIVE CLOUD OF WAVE-SPIT BLOWING PAST HIS HEAD AND SHOULDERS. PLUS HE WAS CHARISMATIC AND GOOD-LOOKING—A DAMN HARD SURFER TO LOOK AWAY FROM.

ANDY IRONS, INDONESIA, 2000.

AERIAL SURFING

In the 1980s, nobody in surfing was as pedigreed as Christian Fletcher: he was the son of 1966 World Championships semifinalist Herbie Fletcher, who led the longboard revival; the grandson of Walter Hoffman, California's original hardcore big-wave rider; and a nephew to two-time world champion Joyce Hoffman. In 1983, Christian Fletcher was a cheerful thirteen-year-old master of both the longboard and shortboard. He also did a lot of skateboarding and was fascinated by that sport's expanding catalog of aerial tricks, as well as its grungy punk-influenced "skate and destroy" aesthetic.

Fletcher dropped out of high school as a freshman and worked on transferring all his skateboard moves to surfing. He wasn't the sport's first aerialist. But he was the first aerial sensation. Magazine photos showed Fletcher levitating four, six, even eight feet above the crest, feet spread wide across his board, arms extended, mouth agape, and eyes slightly bugged. *Surfer* put him on the cover twice in the same twelve-month period, and *Surfing* put him on once, too, for good measure.

Fletcher also turned the aerialist into a surfing outlaw. In 1986, he'd been a quiet Leif Garrett-like pretty boy. Four years later he was a tattooed and pierced surf-death-rocker, with a mohawk and a quiver of boards covered in pentagrams, skulls, and daggers—although never in such a way as to obscure his sponsor logos. He made shrewd use of the outrageous quote. "Fuck the world before it fucks you" was an early, typical effort. Asked where he'd like to be at the turn of the century, Fletcher once replied: "Sitting on an island in the South Pacific with a big fat joint in my mouth."

CHRISTIAN FLETCHER, TRESTLES, 1988.

Hawaii was always the place to go for big surf. That began changing in the 1980s, with the discovery of a big-wave break called Killers in Baja. Then came Maverick's. Located twenty-five miles south of San Francisco, Maverick's had long been the private big-wave domain for a terse Half Moon Bay carpenter named Jeff Clark. For nearly fifteen years, beginning in 1975, Clark invited local surfers to paddle out with him, describing the Maverick's wave as "better than Waimea." Everybody declined. Finally, in 1990, a few local surfers joined Clark and quickly learned that Maverick's was every bit as terrifying as they'd thought: thick, hollow, rocky, often fogged-in, and located on the eastern edge of the "red triangle," known to have to California's highest concentration of great white sharks.

Surfer gave Maverick's a formal introduction in 1992, with a cover story titled "Cold Sweat." A kind of second coming-out took place two years later, after a long, photogenic, and ultimately tragic run of winter surf. Joining the locals, three of Hawaii's top Waimea riders—Brock Little, Mark Foo, and Ken Bradshaw—all paddled out at Maverick's on Friday, December 23, 1994. Just before noon, about three hours into what Brock Little later described as a "relaxing day" of big-wave surfing, Mark Foo lost his balance while dropping into a steep fifteen-footer, belly-flopped, and vanished as the curl pitched into the trough. It wasn't an especially bad-looking wipeout, and nobody thought to check to see if Foo came up. Later that afternoon, a boat full of surfers heading from the Maverick's channel back to Pillar Point Harbor came upon Foo's body floating near the breakwater, the back section of his broken board still leashed to his ankle. The surfers tried to revive Foo, as did the harbor paramedics, but he'd been dead for nearly two hours. It was believed that either his board or leash had gotten snagged on the bottom, and Foo drowned before he could free himself. Foo's death made international news, and Maverick's, for better and worse, was on the map.

JEFF CLARK, MAVERICK'S, 1992.

"MOST OF THE BEST SURFERS AT MAVERICK'S WERE FROM NEARBY SANTA CRUZ, AND INCLUDED A RANGY BIG-WAVE STYLIST NAMED PETER MEL, 16-YEAR-OLD ROOKIE JAY MORIARITY, AND A TOUGH LITTLE REPROBATE NAMED DARRYL "FLEA" VIROSTKO, MASTER OF THE AIR-DROP TAKEOFF, AND THE CASUALLY OFFENSIVE REMARK."

DARRYL "FLEA" VIROSTKO.

TOW SURFING

In 1992, three surfers from Hawaii—
Buzzy Kerbox, Laird Hamilton, and
Darrick Doerner—began using an
inflatable boat to tow themselves into
waves, and in doing so they reinvented
big-wave surfing. Up until then, thirty-
foot waves had long been recognized as
big-wave surfing's top end. Beyond that,
the dangers and difficulties of surfing
were overwhelming. Paddling out was a
nightmare. Holding position in the lineup
was nearly impossible. Then, to actually
catch a thirty-five-foot wave, you had to
use a long, thick, fast-paddling piece of
equipment that looked more like a single
scull racing boat than a surfboard. Using
motorized assistance, and building on the
early experiments of a few others, Kerbox
and his friends quickly refined tow surfing
in giant waves. They traded the inflatable
boat for a Jet Ski, reduced the size of their
boards, and made their base of operations
on Maui, near a fearsome big-wave break
called Jaws. Within two years they were
riding waves half-again as big as anything
ever surfed. Even better, by using shorter
boards, they could perform on the huge
faces, rather than just survive. "You can't
even fuckin' believe the speed," Doerner
rhapsodized, early in the tow era. "And
the distance. The wall stretches out a mile
long in front of you. The wave is twice
as big as Waimea, and five times better.
Fifty-yard bottom turns. Fifty-yard top
turns. Close your eyes and mind-surf
that, man. It's a totally different world out
there."

*TOW-SURF LAUNCH, LAIRD HAMILTON AND DARRICK
DOERNER IN THE BOAT, BUZZY KERBOX RIDING,
NORTH SHORE, 1992.*

THROUGHOUT THE 1990s, TOW SURFING BECAME THE SPORT'S APOLLO PROGRAM, AND LAIRD HAMILTON WAS ITS NEIL ARMSTRONG. IN A SINGLE *MEN'S JOURNAL* ARTICLE, HE WAS DESCRIBED AS BOTH "THE GREATEST SURFER EVER" AND THE "WORLD'S GREATEST ATHLETE." OR AS ONE OF HAMILTON'S BIG-WAVE PEERS SAID, "THERE'S LAIRD, AND THERE'S THE REST OF US."

LAIRD HAMILTON.

SLABS: SHIPSTERN BLUFF

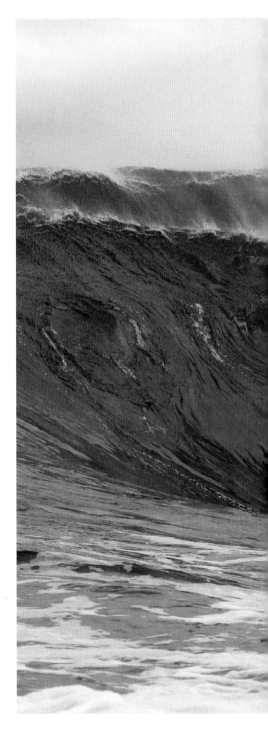

Bigger waves weren't surfing's only new thrill option. Tow surfers were soon heavily engaged in "slab riding," and this warped the big-wave game into something entirely different. At slab breaks like Shipstern Bluff in Tasmania and Ours in Sydney, surfing wasn't so much about the wave's height as the gnarl. Slabs were extra-powerful mashed-together waves that looked like nothing so much as a two-story piece of Frank Gehry architecture. Most had two or three steps in the face. There were multiple curl lines, some running on a bias. All were incredibly shallow and powerful. In fact, for decades paddle surfers had been riding "ledge" waves—scaled-down versions of the slab—but most slabs were regarded as tow-in breaks. Tow or paddle, a surfer rarely dropped down the face with the intention of doing anything but running spear-like through the wave's guts. In that respect, the slab was a throwback to big-wave riding in its original form: surfing as pure survival. There was a fundamental difference, however. As big-wave pioneer Rick Grigg once put it, describing what it was like to sit in the lineup at Waimea or Makaha, "You'd be out there just scared to death—but also completely knocked out by the beauty of it all." Slabs were ugly. Places like Shipstern Bluff, as one surf writer put it, were "so malformed they hardly deserve a name."

SHIPSTERN BLUFF, TASMANIA, 2007.

SURFING IN MUSEUMS, THEATERS, NEWSSTANDS, AND MALLS

During the 1990s, the mainstream media at last came to view surfing as a permanent cultural fixture. No formal announcement, or single event, marked this shift. But more or less all at once, newspapers and magazines, novelists and documentary filmmakers, Hollywood studios and New York publishing houses—everybody seemed to decide that surfing was no longer a novelty or curiosity and that the potential audience for surfing stories now included everyone. Did this mean that the type of surf stories changed? Not really. Violence and danger had always been the mainstream media's favorite surf tropes, and that remained true. For instance, the three biggest surf stories of the 1990s and early 2000s were Mark Foo's death at Maverick's, "surf rage" localism, and thirteen-year-old Hawaiian surfer Bethany Hamilton's return to the water just a few weeks after a tiger shark bit off her left arm in 2003.

Yet the sport appeared in places where it had long been conspicuously absent. Art galleries staged surfing exhibitions. Newspaper travel sections ran articles on exotic locations where good surf was the main draw. Surf documentaries played at Sundance. Famous surfers made the obituaries; when Mickey Dora died of pancreatic cancer in 2002, both the *Los Angeles Times* and the *London Times* published full-length notices.

"SURF CULTURE: THE ART HISTORY OF SURFING," 2002 LAGUNA ART MUSEUM INSTALLATION.

BRAZIL

In the 1980s, Brazil rose to the top tier of surfing nations—a phenomenon that seemed to miniaturize all other international developments in the sport during the period. Brazil caught many Americans and Australians by surprise. The country had never been much of a surf travel destination, and like Japan, it posed a language barrier for the English-speaking surf-world powers. Nevertheless, Brazilian surfers—mostly the upper-class sons of Rio diplomats, financiers, and industrialists—had been hitting it hard since Australian Peter Troy gave an impromptu wave-riding demonstration at Arpoador Beach in 1964. The country offered some real advantages to the surfer: it was warm all year, the waves were small but rarely altogether flat, and there was plenty of room. Also, beachgoing, fitness, and public display were all national obsessions—surfing combined all three. From the beginning, Brazilian surfers were serious about competition. The model, of course, was the Brazilian national soccer team, with its stockpile of World Cup trophies and its roster of legendary players, past and present. Soccer—along with Formula One racing, another Brazilian specialty—gave surfers a huge dose of national sporting pride and a sense of destiny. The surf competition machinery was soon in place. By 1988, Brazil had two events on the world tour schedule, a thriving homegrown surfwear industry, a first-rate national pro tour, and a sound amateur system. By the end of the decade, the country had its first two major world tour stars, Fabio Gouveia and Flavio Padaratz, both of whom would go on to world tour, top-ten year-end finishes.

The big breakthrough came in 2014, when a steely-eyed twenty-year-old goofy-footer from Sao Paulo named Gabriel Medina, in the final event of the year at Pipeline, earned Brazil its first pro circuit world title. It wasn't just Medina. Three or four of his countryman were already on his level, and dozens more—school-age kids, mostly—currently wait in the wings. From now on, all world title talk will be conducted, at least in part, in Portuguese.

GABRIEL MEDINA OF BRAZIL, 2014 WORLD CHAMPION.

JOEL TUDOR

In the early 1990s Joel Tudor emerged as a child prodigy longboarder. Freckled and thin, with a helium-pitched voice, he had, by age fifteen, the smoothest longboarding touch of anyone since David Nuuhiwa. He won two longboarding world championships (in 1998 and 2004) but resisted being categorized. By the late 1990s he was devoting half of his water time to shortboards—all carefully replicated from the late sixties and seventies. As the sport's first and coolest proponent of retro-chic, Tudor decorated his life with artifacts from the past: he drove a '64 Chevy Bel Air with period surf racks bolted to the roof, listened to Charlie Parker, wore bell-bottoms, burned incense, and cut his hair in a Wayne Lynch *Evolution* shag.

Cynics happily gnawed away at the Tudor image, starting with the mind-expanding fact that the average retail price for a Joel Tudor Surfboard noserider—with soulful hand-lettered decals and backyard-style abstract finish—was a cool $1,050. Yet Tudor made no bones about being a professional. If he could ride a trend as well as he could ride a First Point Malibu peeler—well, that's how the game is played.

JOEL TUDOR, EARLY RETRO PERIOD, 1999.

SEXISM, HOMOPHOBIA, AND THE FEMALE SURFER

Women's surfing in the twenty-first century continued to be a fascinating mix of progress, sexism, achievement, and struggle. A cheerful Aussie pro named Layne Beachley dominated the world tour in the post-Lisa Andersen years, winning seven world titles, starting in 1998. Nobody could touch Beachley for range. She was quick and nimble in beachbreak waves and fearless on the North Shore. In 2001, while tow surfing with boyfriend Ken Bradshaw at Outside Log Cabins, Beachley became the first woman to crack the thirty-foot mark. At the same time, Rochelle Ballard and Keala Kennelly, a pair of firewalking haole-Hawaiians, not only became the two best female tube-riders, they helped broaden the image of the female surfer. Ballard, freckled and moon-faced, with short wash-and-go hair—a board-riding "Smurfette," as described by a friend—was the tomboy antidote to the Roxy Girl. She was cute but low-glam, and the sport loved her for it. Kennelly, a rave club DJ with spiky bleach-white hair, didn't quite come out and say she was gay or bisexual, but she told surf journalist Matt George, for the record, that "it took a woman to finally make a woman out of me." Like Ballard, she reaped nothing but appreciation. "Surf fans really do see themselves in their icons," *Surfer*

magazine pointed out, adding that Kennelly's high rank proved that surfers were "a lot more open-minded" than they were given credit for.

Indeed, surf-world homophobia, like sexism, at times seemed to be in retreat. A handful of ex-pro tour women came out of the closet, and in 2007 MTV aired a Los Angeles-based reality series called *Curl Girls*, about a group of lesbian surfers. One year later, a former ASP backbencher named Matt Branson posed for the cover of *Stab* magazine as a well-tattooed, pierced, head-shaved, openly gay man—the first male pro to come out.

Meanwhile, a small number of women surfers, epitomized by pro tour B-league pro Alana Blanchard of Hawaii, built their reputations almost solely on their thong-decorated backsides, and the better-paid women pros were more often than not the ones who showed the most skin in the various "Hottest Women Athletes" magazine and online features. These remain the tricky sexist waters that the next generation of women pros—Stephanie Gilmore, Carissa Moore, Courtney Conlogue, and Sally Fitzgibbons, among others—have to navigate.

AUSTRALIA'S STEPHANIE GILMORE, 2008.

IT FEELS GOOD TO BE A MEMBER OF A SPORTING CONFEDERACY STOCKED WITH CHAMPIONS, ZEALOTS, AND NUTJOBS. SURFERS DRAW PRIDE FROM THE FACT THAT THEIR SPORT HAS LEFT A DISTINCT IMPRINT ON THE WORLD. THERE IS APPRECIATION, TOO, FOR THE FACT THAT WAVE-RIDING, A CENTURY INTO ITS MODERN ERA, IS STILL VERY MUCH A WORK IN PROGRESS.

SUPERBANK, QUEENSLAND, 2005.

ACKNOWLEDGMENTS

I don't have the math skills to even begin to calculate how many people contributed to the making of this book. Special platinum-level thanks to Jeff Divine, Nick Carroll, Grant Ellis, Jeff Hall, Tim DeLaVega, Tom Adler, Steve and Debbee Pezman, and Michael Warshaw. Thanks also to Patrick Moser, Al Hunt, Tom Keck, John Severson, Tony Butt, Mark Fragale, Steve Wilkings, Barry Haun, Anna Trent Moore, Evan Slater, Marcus Sanders, Ben Marcus, Joel Smith, Nathan Myers, Felipe Pomar, Brad Barrett, Dick Metz, Drew Kampion, Glenn Hening, Jamie Tierney, John Elwell, Paul Holmes, Sean Collins, Sam George, Ricky Irons, Miguel Plaza, and John Grannis.

My deepest appreciation to copyeditor Jeff Campbell—every page is better for your efforts. Sarah Malarkey at Chronicle Books made this project happen: she cut the deal, pushed or coddled as necessary, and kept up a steady stream of foul one-liners—a million thanks. I'm indebted to designers Jake Gardner and Ben Kither, and everybody else at Chronicle Books. A deep bow to my agent Wendy Burton-Brouws: we've been a team for ten years now, and I shudder to think how much less of a career this would have been without your help.

Dedicated, with love, to Jodi.

PHOTO AND ILLUSTRATION CREDITS

Author's Note: I did my best to track down the "unknown" photographers and artists whose work is featured in the early part of this book, but in most cases I came up with nothing. Any information about these photographers can be sent to Chronicle Books, care of *The History of Surfing*.

INDEX

A

Abellira, Reno, 177
Aerial surfing, 218, 244
Aikau, Clyde, 233
Aikau, Eddie, 177, 228, 229, 233
Aipa, Ben, 204, 205
Alaia boards, 24, 25, 34, 35
Ala Moana, 168-69
Alter, Hobie, 106, 107
American Pro Championships, 190-91
Andersen, Lisa, 236-37, 241
Anderson, Simon, 206, 207
Anderson, William, 29
Apartheid, 224
Archbold, Matt, 218
Arpoador Beach, 258
Atlantic Surf magazine, 130
August, Robert, 140
Australia. *See also individual locations*
  boardmakers in, 92, 147
  dominance by, 129, 147, 166, 216
  early surfing in, 48, 50
  localism and, 160
  shortboards in, 147, 149, 158
  Summer Olympics (1956) in, 92
Avalon, Frankie, 122, 123
Avalon Beach, 92

B

Backdoor, 198, 199
Baker, Bernie, 183
Baker, Tim, 222
Bali, 184
Ball, John "Doc," 60
Ballard, Rochelle, 262
Bartholomew, Wayne, 166, 196, 197, 198
Bartlett, Charles, 38
Beach Blanket Bingo, 12, 122
Beachboys, 46-47, 57
Beachley, Layne, 262
Beach Party, 122
Bells Beach, 158, 159, 196, 197, 206
Berge, Roar, 226
Bertlemann, Larry, 168-69
Biarritz, 227
Big-wave surfing, 15, 65, 87, 88, 228, 233, 247, 250, 254

Billabong, 216, 227
Blake, Tom, 4, 8, 52, 53, 54, 55, 116
Blanchard, Alana, 262
Bondi Beach, 129
Boren, Lew, 208
Boyer, Lynn, 195
Bradshaw, Ken, 11, 233, 247, 262
Branson, Matt, 262
Brazil, 258
Brewer, Dick, 152
Briggs, Barney, 112
Brown, Bruce, 94, 140, 182
Brown, Woody, 65, 72
Browne, Bud, 94, 95
Byron Bay, 150, 151, 164

C

Caballitos, 18, 19
Cairns, Ian, 192, 221
California. *See also individual locations*
  in the Depression, 53, 58, 60
  introduction of surfing to, 45
  localism and, 160
  longboarding and, 204
  surf contests in, 188
Carroll, Corky, 3, 8, 188, 189
Carroll, Nick, 216
Carroll, Tom, 212, 213, 216, 224, 241
Chicama, 226-27
Clark, Jeff, 246, 247
Club Waikiki, 91
Cocoa Beach, 130, 131, 241
Conlogue, Courtney, 262
Contests, 116, 188, 192, 195, 196, 221. *See also* Professional surfing; *individual contests*
Cook, Captain James, 26, 31, 32
Cooke, Alec, 230-31, 232, 233
Cross, Dickie, 72, 98
Curl Girls, 262
Curren, Pat, 88, 104, 105, 212
Curren, Tom, 212, 214, 215, 218, 220, 221, 224, 241

D

Dale, Dick, 122
David, Vetea, 226

Delaney, Bill, 198
De la Rosa, Luis Miguel "Magoo," 226
Deneuve, Catherine, 91
De Rosnay, Joël, 91
Divine, Jeff, 152
Doerner, Darrick, 233, 250, 251
Dogny, Carlos, 91
Dora, Mickey, 12, 120, 121, 139, 257
Downing, George, 87, 88
Duke Kahanamoku Invitational/ Classic, 188, 189, 228
Durban, 224, 225

E

East Coast (U.S.), 130
East Coast Surfing Championships, 130
Edwards, Phil, 124, 125, 129, 166, 172
Elkerton, Gary, 216, 217
El Salvador, 182-83
Endless Summer, 94, 140, 141, 182

F

Face height, 15
Farrelly, Midget, 8, 128, 129, 147, 149, 152, 188, 276
Fiji, 222
First Point, 82-83
Fitzgerald, Terry, 166, 167
Fitzgibbons, Sally, 262
Fletcher, Christian, 218, 244, 245
Fletcher, Herbie, 244
Florida, 130
Foo, Mark, 233, 247, 257
France, 91, 214, 227
Free Ride, 198
Freeth, George, 44, 45, 118
Froiseth, Wally, 65, 68, 87, 88
Funicello, Annette, 122, 123

G

George, Matt, 12, 262
George, Sam, 238
Gidget. See also Kohner, Kathy "Gidget"
  book, 102